Papa's Legacy:
A Leadership Parable

Michael J. Stabile, Ph.D

FutureNow
CONSULTING

Empowering | Equipping | Transforming
Thinking | Leaders | Cultures
...one person at a time.

Copyright © 2013 Michael J. Stabile

FutureNow Consulting, LLC

Printed in the United States of America

ISBN:0615746888
ISBN-13: 978-0615746883 (FutureNow Consulting, LLC)

DEDICATION

Leaving a legacy of succession is first and foremost on the heart of a Servant Leader. To serve is to lead. The following pages are dedicated to the reader who is willing to hear and see the power of living as a servant leader.

To Jonas Michael, Nolan Joseph, Lucy Kay, Sophia Marie Gloria, and my future grandchildren: you have been the inspiration for writing this book. This is Papa's legacy to you. I pray that as you mature, you, too, will come into your 'sweet spot'. You are the seeds, you are my garden, and your generation and succeeding generations need the treasure of your unique potential.

To the readers, my hope is that this book will not just be information to think about, but it will touch your heart and be used to stimulate, inspire, and transform.

As always, to my Lord and King Jesus Christ, for His glory and honor!

CONTENTS

ACKNOWLEDGMENTS

In the development of any work there are a team of people who are influential and willing to serve selflessly. I would like to express my sincere thanks to Tom Highly who challenged my thinking about the characters and dialogue. To my editor, Benjamin Dougherty, who used his gifts and talents to edit the text without changing or diminishing my voice and vision. To Brian Warren, a gifted artist and graphic designer, your cover design and other works of art truly are inspirational. Finally, to my lovely bride, Pam, you are my constant encourager who inspires me to continually unleash my potential and "sweet spot."

INTRODUCTION

Why this book?

This book is about leaving a leadership legacy. It is about the transformational impact one person can have on generations. It is about inspiring an army of ordinary people to lead by serving. Robert Greenleaf, who coined the phrase "servant leadership", proposed, "to serve is to lead." Real leadership is about serving others. It is not about a unique or special kind of human being, but about ordinary people who have been created to do extraordinary things. Therefore, everyone has the potential for leadership because everyone can choose to have a positive influence. As John Maxwell, leadership writer and speaker, expounds, "leadership is influence; nothing more and nothing less." A servant leader has the influence or authority to transform cultures "one person at a time." Further, author and speaker Myles Monroe makes this thought provoking statement, "The abortion of potential is the death of the future."

Consider, if you will, all of us, in one-way or another (good or bad) will have an impact and influence for at least 100 years. Yes, 100 years! The next and future generations need the treasure of our influence. We must not rob a generation(s) of the wealth that each one of us possesses. Your influence and legacy is passed down or caught by everyone with whom you make contact and with whom your life intersects, especially your children, grandchildren, and even great grandchildren. What they see modeled, demonstrated, exemplified, talked about, or taught gets planted or embedded in them and passed on to the next generation. I call this "imprinting," building a total context and culture around the message.

The question each of us has to ask is: "How are my actions imprinting others?" This is not a unique idea. In the classic movie, It's a Wonderful Life, Jimmy Stewart's character George Bailey was an ordinary man whose personal sacrifices had real impact and influence on the community and world around him. Blind to his influence and filled with self-pity, he considers taking his own life. Luckily, an angelic messenger shows George a grim picture of what the world would be like without him. George learns that his leadership imprinted everyone around him; the community looked to George's selflessness as a model for their own lives. This book mirrors the same kind of sentiment; directing our ordinary lives to serve others with purposeful, intentional, and habitual influence.

Why a leadership parable?

A parable is defined as a short fictitious story with human characters that illustrates a universal truth or principle. This leadership parable is a "sticky story," which helps the reader to remember the key lessons from the parable, and is intended to create a mental framework about the influence of a servant leader. The underlying truth lesson: "to serve is to lead" is portrayed through the heart-felt relationship between a man and his Papa (grandfather.) This simple story provides an emotional connection and backdrop to help the reader reflect on how servant leadership is more "caught than taught." Therefore, this story creates a mental framework that can challenge and motivate you, the reader, to reflect on your current reality, providing the motivation and inspiration to cultivate your own "garden of influence." Our world is suffering from a lack of leadership, but you can help make a difference. Whether you know it or not, you have the ability within you to lead by serving. Cumulatively, we can create an army of servant leaders, leaving behind a leadership legacy for future generations. Will you be part of Papa's legacy?

THE PROLOGUE

"What was one of the most defining moments in your life?"

Without hesitation, Dr. Jonas K. Nolan, replied, "When I chose to stop living for myself and started serving others."

Surprised and intrigued by his response, the reporter followed up, asking "Was there a particular event, circumstance, or personal encounter that brought you to that defining moment?"

Smiling, Jonas slowly shook his head in affirmation. Jonas thought back to a time and place over 20 years earlier that not only defined his life, but transformed it. It was hard to believe that one moment in time literally changed his life like no other event before or after. Jonas had many influential moments in his life, but the choice he made in that one moment redirected him on a journey, an adventure, from which he never looked back.

Adjusting her glasses, the reporter glanced at her notes. She knew the basic facts of Dr. Nolan's life. Twenty years earlier, Dr. Nolan was a celebrated professor at a prominent university. An author, consultant, and sought after expert in the field of personal and organizational leadership development, he mysteriously resigned his position and joined a movement of leaders committed to transforming cultures one person at a time through servant leadership. At the time, it was a very controversial move, and many of his previous supporters abandoned him, seeing his new beliefs as extremely radical. However, Jonas and a committed fellowship of leaders from all walks of life had persevered to influence the arenas of politics, business, education, media, and religion.

Everywhere they went transformational change would begin to break out. Although there were those who opposed their approach and beliefs, there was no questioning their results. Cultures were being transformed one person at a time. Schools that traditionally had the poorest results and difficulty attracting highly qualified teachers became nationally recognized schools that attracted teachers from across the nation. Businesses that struggled with employee turnover and customer satisfaction became top places to work and do business in their industries. Government officials, many times secretly, called on these transformational leaders in critical situations. Jonas was known for his ability to inspire people to move from being followers to true servant leaders. He had dedicated the last 20 years of his life to studying, applying, and teaching servant leadership.

Taking a sip of water, Jonas finally answered her question. "That defining moment happened at a conference two decades ago, but that moment was an epiphany. It was then that I realized my life's true purpose and the legacy I was destined to leave. You see, until that time, I had been struggling internally, but I wasn't fully aware of why." Jonas' gaze drifted toward the window. "That moment in time brought me to a life changing choice," Jonas replied.

The reporter shifted uncomfortably at Dr. Nolan's words, as she had often struggled with the same sense of internal conflict. Nicole Moss knew she would be a reporter before entering college to study journalism. As a young reporter, she decided to follow the advice of her favorite professor: get the story and get the credit. In the process, she had risen to the position of lead reporter for one of the few newspapers to survive the movement to computer-based news, breaking stories in print and online. The fact that she had to be hard-nosed and slightly cut-throat to get to the top of her profession was expected. This had been an effective if sometimes unpopular strategy, but left her feeling strangely unsatisfied in a way that seemed to resonate with Dr. Nolan's words. Nicole asked, "Can you help me understand what you mean by, 'it brought me to a life changing choice'?"

Dr. Nolan stood up and walked across his office to his crowded bookshelves as he spoke. "Until that point, I thought that I was at the center of the universe and realized it was not about me. I came to a crossroad, a moral decision point, when I was confronted with the truth about myself and I needed to do something about it. It's like this: most of us never really get past our twos. We are all very self-centered, and we demand that everything and everyone around us meet our needs."

Dr. Nolan took down a picture of his granddaughter from the bookshelf and brought it back to show Nicole. The grinning image of the precocious blond toddler in a yellow sun hat brought a smile to Nicole's face.

"She's adorable," Nicole said.

"My granddaughter, Lucy. Two years old last month," Dr. Nolan said with a chuckle. Nicole handed him back the picture as he continued, "Two year olds can be like dictators. It's their way or the highway. They'll cry, scream, hit, and bite, until they get their way. The thing is, most of us never get past our twos because we are basically selfish. When I said, I made a life changing choice, I mean I finally realized I needed to stop being selfish and grow up. I needed to be who I was really meant to be."

"And who are you really meant to be?" Nicole asked.

Placing Lucy's picture on the end table next to him, Jonas sat down in the aging leather wingback chair across from Nicole, smiled, and confidently said, "I was born to serve and to continue the legacy of servant leadership!"

Nicole looked down at her notebook to hide her surprised reaction. Again the simplicity and conviction of his answer made her take pause. Fighting off a tinge of envy at Dr. Nolan's self assuredness, she circled his last words, "I was born to serve and to continue the legacy of servant leadership!"

After a moment, Nicole looked up and asked, "Dr. Nolan, how did you come to that conclusion?"

1 THE BEST AND WORST OF TIMES

Standing in the wings of the auditorium, Dr. Jonas K. Nolan couldn't help but smile as he listened to the host introduce him as the keynote speaker to the annual meeting of the International Council on Leadership. It was a climactic day for Jonas and his family. His life long body of work, research, and teaching had brought him to this pinnacle event. Over the years, a Who's Who of the most inspirational, motivational, and influential experts on leadership had been asked to give the keynote address to this most prestigious group of international leaders. Now, Jonas Nolan was being added to this elite group. With all that said, it certainly was one of the best times in his life. His wife, children, mother, and father were in the crowd and were overwhelmed with this great honor. To many, speaking as the keynote at the International Council on Leadership was the ultimate award in his chosen field of individual and organizational leadership development.

Standing next to him, the stage manager whispered "Man! Packed house! Hope you know what you're talking about…" Jonas chuckled, "So do I!" However, in those brief moments before he walked up to the speaker's podium, he couldn't help but wonder, "What would Papa say about all of this?" Papa, the loving name he called his grandfather, had been a very successful and influential leader in his own right. However, the International Council on Leadership had never allowed him the privilege of speaking, presenting his research, or giving the keynote at this conference. Many, especially the current advisory board, felt his message and body of work, to use their words, was too archaic, simplistic, and unrealistic.

To a large extent, he agreed with the many. Jonas had made that clear to Papa years before. A week after receiving his Ph.D. in Leadership Thought and Practice, his wife threw a celebration party for the family at their home. Standing alone at the punchbowl in the backyard, Papa approached Jonas with a smile.

"Jonas, I am so proud of you." Papa clapped him on the back "By the way do you know what Ph.D. stands for? Piled higher and deeper." Papa laughed. Jonas had to laugh along with him. Sometimes the life of an academic seemed to require a pitchfork rather than a pen.

"I am so proud of you, Jonas K. Nolan! The man! You will do great things!"

Jonas blushed. "Thank you, Papa. I'm going to give it my best." Papa paused and looked upward, but it was the kind of pause Jonas had experienced thousands of times before. It was the sort of pregnant pause Papa always used to add dramatic effect. As always, the pause was followed by a sly grin spreading across his face.

"Jonas, I've been waiting for this day since you were born. You are a special young man and God has given you great potential, but with great potential comes great responsibility. In my heart, I know you are the one to carry on my legacy and work." Papa laid a warm hand on Jonas's shoulder. "What I've started, I want you to continue, because I know you will do greater things than me." Jonas struggled to understand what he meant by greater. "Jonas, will you join together with me? We can change the world one person at a time."

Jonas had been dreading this moment for years. He saw it coming. Papa was a good, humble man who impacted many over the years. But his work and his message were archaic and a world away from what Jonas studied and poured his life into through graduate studies and his dissertation. Papa was not in touch with the modern world. His old fashioned approach to leadership theory, practice, and development didn't seem to fit in with the fast paced highly corporate world in which Jonas lived. He cringed.

"Papa I ah, ah, am honored, but…" Jonas paused, remembering that Papa once told him, "whenever a conjunction like "but" is used, it negates everything that proceeds it." After that, Jonas couldn't really remember what he said; his rationale, his dreams, his aspirations, were a blur of weak excuses. All he remembered was the look of disappointment on Papa's face! Small tears replaced the twinkle in Papa's eyes.

At the time, Jonas reassured himself that he had made the

right decision. Dr. Nolan had been offered a position at a prestigious university that was going to fund his research and allow him to continue the work he had started in his dissertation. He was going to lecture, write books, and become famous based on the theories he developed. A publisher had already expressed interest in a book based on his research. Jonas was on the fast track to fame and fortune. What his grandfather was offering, at that time, seemed so meager and insignificant.

Papa took a moment, cleared his throat, and regained his composure. Dipping out a glass of punch, Papa said, "Jonas, like I said, you will do great things." Papa looked directly into Jonas's eyes, and thought "but it will take years for your heart to catch up with your head."

Papa continued, "Greatness is what you are looking for, but the greatest among you is one who serves. Jonas, to lead is to serve. The study of leadership is a great and noble undertaking, but studying, theorizing, and building models are not real leadership. Remember, real leadership begins with the natural feeling that one wants to serve. To serve must be first. You are focused on being the leader-first. The leader-first mentality is motivated by power, position, material possessions, or prestige. The difference is servant leaders make sure other people's legitimate needs are served. Jonas, what are you trying to do?"

"What are you trying to do?" Jonas always found that question to be one of the easiest to ask and most difficult to answer.

Like a bolt of lightning, the question brought him back to the moment, back to the reality of his keynote address.

"What am I trying to do?" Jonas pondered.

He self-reflected, "I have taught hundreds of classes at the university. My students adhere to and respect my teaching and theories. I have published articles, written books, created leadership models, and have made a name for myself. I am considered a leadership expert. On the speaking circuit, I can name my fee anywhere I am invited to speak. The university has given me the authority to run the new leadership Center. I am the chair of the department, and nothing happens in my department without my approval. I have lived the "American dream"; I have cars, homes, travel the world, etc. I am a good person. I give to charities. I go to church. I help others, and I have a good wife and good children."

At that very moment, Papa's words again ripped through his very being into his heart, "What are you trying to do?" It became very clear to Jonas that he had embraced and been blinded by the 'leader-first' mentality. He had totally conformed to and had been motivated by power, position, possessions, and prestige. The only needs he ever really met were his own selfish desires.

The reality hit him so squarely that he said it aloud. "With all of my potential and accomplishments, I've been working in the wrong direction. To serve is to lead. The only person I have served is myself." Jonas realized what Papa was offering him all those years before: the essence of real leadership. Just as he had many years ago, Jonas stood at a crossroads…

"…Ladies and gentleman, Dr. Jonas K. Nolan!" A wave of

thunderous applause erupted in the house. Jonas stood motionless. Abruptly, the stage manager snapped his fingers in front of Jonas's face," Hey! Snap out of it! You're on!" The applause was still thundering as he approached the podium, his palms began to sweat and his heart raced.

Jonas was having a battle of conscience that might cost him everything. All his preparation now came down to a choice of conscience that could change the course of his life and fulfill Papa's legacy. "What am I trying to do?"

2 THE ASSIGNMENT

Before arriving at Dr. Nolan's house for the interview, Nicole Moss had her own battle of conscience. Nicole was driven by ambition, or so she thought. She wanted to be on the fast track, but to her chagrin she felt derailed. Here she was covering a story that at best would wind up hidden in the back pages of the newspaper or in some pretentious life-style magazine section. She longed for headline breaking news, "My voice and talents need to be heard and recognized…", Nicole, now consciously wondered if she said that out loud. This is not my dream: covering some old guy who is a leadership self-help guru. She chuckled to herself, "Maybe he can help me."

"Nicole, I need you to interview a person that I think will be of real interest to our readers," her editor's words still ignited emotion as she felt her face reddening. As much as she protested and argued that a lead reporter should be focused on breaking news, headlines, scandals, investigative reporting, her logical rational arguments did not persuade her editor.

"Nicole, you have an appointment to interview Dr. Jonas K.

Nolan. Now get!" And with those words she reeled on her heels and in one big huff she snatched her coat, purse, and notepad and marched out the door.

On her way to Dr. Nolan's she was lost in her thoughts and wondered, "How did I get to this point in my life?" The last thing she consciously remembered about the drive was looking both ways before leaving the parking garage and then she was driving on automatic pilot.

Nicole was from a very affluent family that focused on reputation, status, opportunity, and most of all the accumulation of wealth. From the time she was very young, her father drilled into her thinking, "Nicole, sit-up straight, suck-in your stomach, walk with pride, and never never embarrass me or our family. You are a Moss, and being a Moss means responsibility and duty!"

"Don't cry, crying is a sign of weakness, never let anybody see you crying. Because you are a woman you will have to work harder to be successful. Be strong, work hard, and do whatever it takes to succeed." Those words still rang in her ears and the voice of her father was always with her.

Nicole suddenly realized that she needed to pay attention to the exit signs to get to Dr. Nolan's. She noticed the crowded highways lightening and the landscape change into the rolling hills of late autumn and the beautiful colors of Fall. She had forgotten how peaceful and calming a drive in the country could be. Dr. Nolan's home was only about 30 minutes outside the city, but it seemed like a world away from the heaviness of urban life.

She saw the exit and turned on to Highway 42. She was looking for landmarks that led to his private drive. The private road was not impressive, but as it wound up the hill to the Nolan home, she could see the simplicity and beauty of this place. It was lined with trees now almost barren, but with the last remnant of leaves. It was an idyllic country setting with a quaint cottage style home surrounded by a white picket fence. There was something about this place that brought on an overwhelming feeling of tranquility and peace.

As she parked the car in the circle drive, Nicole opened the car door and immediately drank in the fragrant smells of the pine trees that encircled the property. She walked up the cobble stone pathway to the front door and rang the doorbell.

3 THE "WAY" BACK HOME

Jonas was conflicted. Time was standing still and he was about to give the biggest speech of his life. In that moment, he had experienced a series of paradoxical thoughts that all began with "if" and ended with "then."

"If I follow my heart, then what will the advisory board think? If I express what I really want to say, then will I ever be able to show myself at a conference like this again? If I share Papa's legacy, then will I lose everything I have worked for all these years? If I change my speech now, then where will I begin?"

Then as the next "If and then" statement was being formulated in his mind, he was overwhelmed by emotion and remembered something Papa had repeated to him as he was growing up.

"Jonas, you have been born with an assignment. The only way you will fulfill that assignment is to be true to who you have been created to be. Great leaders do not desire to lead but to serve. There is a leader in everyone, waiting to be released. It is not if you are a leader, but how you are a leader. Will you discover and unleash the real leader within you?"

To be honest, he had never really understood what Papa meant until this very moment. I have an assignment and unique journey that has led me to this crossroads. The question is not what will I do but what must I do, now? How can I best serve, now?

Papa was a man who walked his talk and modeled what he taught in the ordinary activities of life. A professor, Dr. Howard Hendricks, made a deep impression on Papa with this quote: "If you want others to bleed, you must be willing to hemorrhage." In others words, more is caught than taught. People just don't want to hear your words; they want to see the attitudes, actions, and behaviors that support them. You can't just say the words; they must come from your attitudes, beliefs, and commitments.

Papa would often say, "Are you seeking to serve others or yourself?" He would point first to himself and repeat, "I am progressing, but I am not perfect. Progression not perfection!" Papa understood he was far from perfect, but he was progressively becoming the message: to serve is to lead.

Jonas Nolan, you are a hypocrite! You are a selfish man. How can you now talk about selfless humility through servant leadership? He agonized. The battle in his mind was intensifying.

Dr. Albert Schweitzer once said, "I don't know what your destiny will be, but one thing I do know. The only ones among you who will be really happy are those who will have sought and found how to serve." Perhaps this was the moment in space, time, and history for service and sacrifice. If servant leadership is influence and influence is built on service, when a person comes to that insight it is not as important as the willingness to act on it. Ken Blanchard, author of the classic The One Minute Manager, puts it this way, "Intentions minus actions equal squat." All the good intentions in the world don't mean a thing if they don't line up with our actions. However, "intentions plus actions equal will." It is only when our actions are aligned with our intentions that we become consistent and congruent leaders. There was no question in Jonas' mind about his intention, but the issue now was held in his will. Would he, by his actions, serve?

One of Papa's favorite quotes that he would use in his training sessions or lectures came from *A Return to Love* by Marianne Williamson (a quote sometimes erroneously attributed to Nelson Mandela's inaugural speech):

> *"Our deepest fear is not that we are inadequate. Our deepest fear is that we are powerful beyond measure. It is our light not our darkness, that most frightens us. We ask ourselves, who am I to be brilliant, gorgeous, talented and famous? Actually, who are you not to be? You are a child of God. You playing a small part doesn't serve the world. There is nothing enlightened about shrinking so that other people won't feel insecure around you. We are born to magnify the glory of God that is within us. It is not just in some of us; it's in everyone. And as we let our own light shine, we unconsciously give other people permission to do the same. As we are liberated from our fear, our presence automatically liberates others."*

Could it be my deepest fear is now being exposed and being

brought to light? Is it now time for me to unleash the true leader within? Is it time to journey into my destiny and assignment for being born? Is it time to be liberated from my real fear?

Every journey begins with a first step. Jonas was now contemplating a step of faith that he never dreamed he would even be confronted with, especially at a time such as this. Where do I even begin and how am I going to find the right words to express what is passionately moving in my heart?

What would Papa say and do if he were standing here right now? As Jonas pondered that thought, immediately a calming peace came over him. What would Papa do? That's simple, I know exactly what Papa would say if he were in my place addressing this audience.

Jonas flashed to a vivid memory. He was 13 years old and Papa invited him to a conference where he was giving a workshop in San Diego, California. The experience was so vivid because Papa demonstrated his love for him throughout his life by his actions. Papa's love was an attitude that was displayed in how he treated people. He always made you feel like you were the most important person in the world. He showed tremendous patience during that trip and gave special attention to a young man who was feeling awkward in his own skin during puberty. At times, Jonas felt like Papa was the only one that ever really heard and got him. Everyone he encountered felt his words of encouragement and appreciation. He went out of his way to treat others with respect and tried to meet their legitimate needs not their wants. People just felt they were of great value when they were around Papa. He gave them the dignity that they deserved not necessarily earned.

Jonas remembers, I watched and drank in every encounter Papa had with people at the conference. Whether he was speaking to a group or privately talking to individuals, Papa was always the same. He was a man who brought 'light' to everyone he encountered.

In one of the workshop sessions, Papa exhorted the group with these words, "The way back home always begins with humility. Just like the parable of the Prodigal Son, selfish pride keeps us from realizing who and what we really are. **Humility is the ability to be you.** The word comes from the Latin word "humus", meaning earth. **Humility denotes earthiness or an awareness of one's true essence.** Being humble, therefore, does not mean degrading or reducing oneself in the estimation of another, but rather **having an awareness, acceptance, and appreciation of one's true worth and value.** Humility is not self-serving, but selfless service. It is the opposite of selfish ambition–ambition does not take others into account. Thus, one cannot decide to be humble because it is not something you decided to be; it is what you are. **Servant Leaders are individuals who have or are in the process of discovering their true selves and know who they are.** Therefore, true servant leaders are naturally humble, in the full sense of the word.

With conviction, Jonas repeats, **"The way back home always begins with humility."** Like the prodigal son, I dismissed my real destiny and went on my own road to success, fame, and fortune, but in the end I am empty. I have woken up in the "pig pen" of my own making. My selfish pride has interfered with the unleashing of my true worth and value. Pride does come before the fall.

Where do I begin... it is clear, with my journey to humility, the way back home!

4 THE LION AMONG SHEEP

"What happened next, how did you begin the keynote address?" Nicole's questions brought Jonas back to the present abruptly. His reflection stirred up all the emotions and feelings from that day over 20 years ago.

"The journey of 1,000 miles always begins with the first step. My first step, at the time, was a huge leap. I came to a crossroads of conscience and heart belief. I remembered and memorized a story Papa had told me when I was a young boy. The story was from a book by Dr. Myles Monroe. Papa said this one story helps all of us understand where we must begin. A decision today to affect the future begins when we get a glimpse of our 'true self' and then choose. You have to evaluate your past and your potential and step toward one or the other."

Jonas stepped up to the podium and after he gave some introductory remarks and thanked the advisory council for asking him to speak at this conference he said, "I must apologize, but I am not going to deliver my prepared speech as it was listed in the program."

Jonas could feel drops of sweat forming on his forehead and his heart began to beat faster within his chest so that his pulse was audible. As he scanned the audience, he felt the pressure of thousands of eyes staring right thorough him. And briefly as he paused he was wondering what they were thinking.

"In fact, I am not going to talk about anything from my previous lectures or books. Tonight, I want to talk to you about a decision I am about to make and a choice that goes back to a conversation I had many years ago with my grandfather, whom I lovingly call Papa. This is about a personal journey. My Papa told me a story that he took from Dr. Myles Monroe's book *The Spirit of Leadership*. Until just a few minutes ago, I never fully understood how this story would change my life."

"There was once a farmer who lived in this village and also was a herder of sheep. One day, he took his sheep out to pasture, and while they were grazing, he suddenly heard a strange noise coming from a patch of grass, which first sounded like a kitten. Led by his curiosity, the old shepherd went to see what was the source of this insistent sound, and to his surprise, he found a lone shivering lion cub, obviously separated from his family. His first thought was the danger he would be in if he stayed too close to the cub and his parents returned. So the old man quickly left the area and watched from a distance to see if the mother lion or the pack would return. However, after the sun began to set, and there was still no activity to secure the lion cub, the shepherd decided that, in his best judgment, and for the safety and survival of the lion cub, he would take him to his farmhouse and care for him.

THE LION HAD BECOME A SHEEP BY ASSOCIATION.

Over the next eight months, the shepherd hand-fed this cub with fresh milk and kept him warm, safe, and secure in the protective confines of the farmhouse. After the cub had grown into a playful, energetic ball of shiny muscle, he would take him out daily with the sheep to graze. The lion cub grew with the sheep and became a part of the herd. They accepted him as one of their own, and he acted like one of them. After fifteen months had passed, the little cub had become an adolescent lion, but he acted, sounded, responded, and behaved just like one of the sheep. In essence, the lion had become a sheep by association. He had lost himself and become one of them.

One hot day, four years later, the shepherd sat on a rock, taking refuge in the slight shade of a leafless tree. He watched over his flock as they waded into the quiet, flowing water of a river to drink. The lion that thought he was a sheep followed them into the water to drink. Suddenly, just across the river, there appeared out of the thick jungle bush a large beast that the lion cub had never seen before. The sheep panicked and, as if under the spell of some survival instinct, leaped out of the water and dashed toward the direction of the farm. They never stopped until they were all safely huddled behind the fence of the pen. Strangely, the lion cub, which was now a grown lion, was also huddled with them, stricken with fear.

While the flock scrambled for the safety of the farm, the beast made a sound that seemed to shake the forest. When he lifted his head above the tall grass, the shepherd could see that he held in his blood-drenched mouth the lifeless body of a lamb from the flock. The man knew that danger had returned to his part of the forest.

Seven days passed without further incident, and then, while the flock grazed, the young lion went down to the river to drink. As he bent

25

over the water, he suddenly panicked and ran wildly toward the farmhouse for safety. The sheep did not run and wondered why he had, while the lion wondered why the sheep had not run since he had seen the beast again. After a while, the young lion went slowly back to the flock and then to the water to drink again. Once more, he saw the beast and froze in panic. It was his reflection in the water.

While he tried to understand what he was seeing, suddenly, the beast appeared out of the jungle again. The flock dashed with breakneck speed toward the farmhouse, but before the young lion could move, the beast stepped in the water toward him and made that deafening sound that filled the forest. For a moment, the young lion felt that his life was about to end. He realized that he saw not just one beast, but also two— one in the water and one before him.

His head was spinning with confusion as the beast came within ten feet of him and growled at him face-to-face with frightening power in a way that seemed to say to him, "Try it, and come and follow me."

HE FELT STIRRINGS THAT HE HAD NEVER KNOWN BEFORE.

As fear gripped the young lion, he decided to try to appease the beast and make the same sound. However, the only noise that came from his gaping jaws was the sound of a sheep. The beast responded with an even louder burst that seemed to say, "Try it again." After seven or eight attempts, the young lion suddenly heard himself make the same sound as the beast. He also felt stirrings in his body and feelings that he had never known before. It was as if he was experiencing a total transformation in mind, body, and spirit.

As Jonas said these words an overwhelming peace and calm filled his being. It was like he was having an out of body experience. The internal conflict and tension he had experienced just minutes earlier was now being replaced by floods of calm like he had never experienced before.

Suddenly, there stood in the river of life two beasts growling at and to each other. Then the shepherd saw something he would never forget. As the beastly sounds filled the forest for miles around, the big beast stopped, turned his back on the young lion, and started toward the forest. Then he paused and looked at the young lion one more time and growled, as if to say, "Are you coming?" The young lion knew what the gesture meant and suddenly realized that his day of decision had arrived – the day he would have to choose whether to continue to live life as a sheep or to be the self he had just discovered. He knew that, to become his true self, he would have to give up the safe, secure, predictable, and simple life of the farm and enter the frightening, wild, untamed, unpredictable, dangerous life of the jungle. It was a day to become true to himself and leave the false image of another life behind. It was an invitation to a "sheep" to become the king of the jungle. Most importantly, it was an invitation for the body of a lion to possess the spirit of a lion.

After looking back and forth at the farm and the jungle a few times, the young lion turned his back on the farm and the sheep with whom he had lived for years, and he followed the beast into the forest to become who he always had been – a lion king."

Jonas looked directly into the eyes of the audience and with complete confidence exclaimed, "I now understand why my Papa shared and continually repeated this story with me so many years ago. I am the young lion. Today, I am making a decision that will affect the future; I am standing at the river of life and got a glimpse of my true self. Tonight, I am choosing to cross the river. As the young lion got a glimpse of his true self in his reflection at the river, I realize I need to take a step toward my real potential and destiny."

Jonas reflectively paused, looked down, and then took a deep breath, "For too many years, I have spent my life focused on me. I realized that it is time for my heart to catch up with my head. I am a selfish prideful man. The only person I have really ever served has been myself. I wanted to be great, but tonight it is very clear with all my accomplishments, I have built my house upon the sand. I made the study of leadership my life and I tell you all here in this auditorium: that is not real leadership! I, like many of you, have a leader-first mentality. It has been motivated by power, position, material possessions, and prestige. With all of my so-called accomplishments and activities there really has been very little transformational change in the people my life has intersected. Tonight, all of that is going to change!"

Jonas made eye contact with his wife and family, "I have come to grips with my past and can no longer deny my real God-given potential and purpose. I choose to take a step toward becoming my true self. Like the young lion, I am giving up the safe, predictable, and simple life of the farm, and entering the frightening, wild, untamed, unpredictable, dangerous life of the jungle. In other words, I am leaving the safe confines of my self-centered life and am taking the first step toward real leadership. With all of my theories, books, and teaching, my biggest regret is that I failed to recognize *"to serve is to lead."*

5 LIVING PAPA'S LEGACY

"Don't leave me hanging!" Nicole pleaded with Jonas; "How did you end the speech and what was the response?"

Jonas sat back in his chair and chuckled; "I don't remember much of what happened after I spoke those words, but I do remember the reactions of those who heard me that evening. In fact, the look on the faces of some of the members of the advisory council was priceless. It was a cross between shock, astonishment, embarrassment, and anger!"

"As I mentioned, there was the group of leadership experts and gurus, many were a part of the advisory council, who took my speech personally and were very offended by my public declaration. They felt I used this time to make a mockery of the International Council of Leadership and to make them look foolish. To them, I was a fool who literally had just thrown away his career. I think my publisher was among that group. However, I believe she was more concerned about the sale of my books going south and worried that my worth to her had just diminished not only at this conference, but worldwide."

"There were some academics and CEOs who had hailed my books and theories on leadership who felt like they had egg on their faces. They were my 'leadership disciples' or to use another term, groupies; they felt like their leader had just gone off the deep end. They felt that I needed to be committed for treatment. It was obvious to them; I was having a nervous break down and was not in my right mind. It was very interesting; those who would live and die by my theories were now saying my genius had turned to insanity. When it comes right down to the bottom line, they too were only committed to the ideas and the prestige of my popularity at that time."

Jonas took another sip of his coffee glanced at the reporter and smiled to himself. "There was another response that night from a group which seemed encouraging, but over time those comments, too, were shallow and really not genuine. Their comments were flattering, '*O, Dr. Jonas, that was such an inspirational speech*' or '*you really challenged me to make some changes.*' I believe they were sincere and had great intentions, but not enough to be transformational. In fact, I personally followed up with some of the people who made those comments to see if I could help them in their journey. However, like all of us, each one of them had excuses for why they remained in the same place or were continuing the same habits, etc."

"Do you feel there was any lasting impact from the speech you gave that night?" Nicole interjected.

"Yes, there were a few who were on the same journey that I was embarking upon. Some were a little further down the road and others had a more novice understanding, but there was no question that among that crowd was a group who had "seeds" either planted or watered. They were the ones who not only heard my words, but also understood the heart behind them. Out of this group, many close relationships have been developed and maintained over these past 20 years."

The reporter looked down at her notebook and hastily scanned her writing as if she was searching for something. She had been so engaged in the story that she felt herself being drawn in by his words, but reality hit; like those people Jonas had described, she felt as though his story was too good to be true. Her father's words about being careful whom you trust and her years of training as a reporter had taught her to be skeptical and remain rational. How could she say this in a polite but direct way?

Then, she stopped, looked up from her notes and looked down again to help her formulate her next question. "Dr. Jonas, all of this is very interesting, but to be honest, it is hard for me to grasp what your decision and choice was all about. It seems to me like it was a personal moral dilemma. Can you give me more insight into what your decision has cost you?"

Jonas rubbed his chin before he replied, "This may sound like an odd answer, but in one sense it cost me everything, and in another it cost me nothing. Yes, my reputation was controversial at best. I eventually resigned from my position at the university, and my book publisher eventually cancelled my contracts. In the eyes of many, I had given up everything."

He leaned forward and looked directly at Nicole, and she noticed the shift of body posture and how bright and open his eyes were, "However, that night was a watershed moment for me. For the first time that I could remember, I was at peace, at rest. It is the kind of peace that can't really be explained, but it is an inner peace that shouts, 'I have more than enough from the inside out.'"

"Excuse me, Dr. Nolan," the reporter stopped him abruptly.

Jonas looked her directly in the eyes, "Please call me Jonas."

"Ok, Jonas, you had some kind of religious experience or something, right?"

"Ms. Moss, it was more of a life changing experience," Jonas replied.

"Please call me, Nicole", the reporter responded in a tit for tat manner. "If it wasn't a religious experience what would you call it?"

"Nicole, each of us must find our 'sweet spot'. In other words, you must find your unique place in the vast universe of humanity that God has designed for you. Our 'sweet spot' is the place uniquely fit for each of us where we find peace. Imagine earning pay for being at peace or leaving home each day to do what gives you peace, or having more than enough in every circumstance."

"Oh, I get it, this peace is about finding the right job fit," Nicole shot back with a confident look of understanding on her face.

"Nicole, it is far greater than finding the right job. When you discover your 'sweet spot' you begin to live out your unique gifts and talents. You are at home or comfortable with who you are and what you bring to any given situation. When you are in your 'sweet spot', you are moving in the zone of your destiny. In other words, you come alive because you are doing what you do best and what you were uniquely created to do. Nicole, I believe every human being has the potential to live in his or her 'sweet spot'. We were all born with an assignment and a purpose to fulfill."

Again she felt her reporter instincts kick in, even though she was fighting this tug that resonated deep within her. "Tell me more," Nicole encouraged.

With confidence and passion in his voice Jonas continued, "Living out of our 'sweet spot' gives us a maximum life or what I call MAX Life. When we are maximizing our potential for progress, we live a peaceful life from the inside out. Oliver Wendell Holmes said:

> "The biggest tragedy in America is not the great waste of natural resources, though this is tragic. The greatest tragedy is the waste of human resources. The average person goes to his grave with his music still in him." Writer Norman Cousins had a slightly different twist in this thought when he said, "Death isn't the greatest loss in life. The greatest loss is what dies inside of us while we live."

It is like a gigantic six billion piece jigsaw puzzle where many pieces look alike, but in the "big picture" each piece is unique. The shape of our 'sweet spot' has been predetermined and perfectly fit for us. The way the gigantic puzzle was created calls for each piece to be fitted into the spot that it was designed for. Therefore, if we are not in our right 'spot' it impacts and affects the whole picture that is part of the Creator's design. When we are not in our specially designed 'sweet spot' it is like a virus, and it impacts the whole, and will cause disruption and distortion. A virus is a foreign substance that makes the whole body sick; thus, when we are not living in our unique 'sweet spots', it not only affects us, but also impacts the whole of humanity. However, if we discover and are unleashed in our 'sweet spot' it brings MAX Life or peace to us and, in turn, it brings life and peace to all who come in contact with us."

As a reporter, she realized the need to move on with the interview, but Nicole, was drawn more and more by the power of the words Jonas was speaking. "As you reflect from that defining moment, what do you feel has been transformational about your life?"

Immediately Jonas responded, **"We live our lives based on who we think we are.** Just like the story of the *Lion Among Sheep,* if you believe in your heart that you are a sheep, then you will stay in the confines that others have placed you in or that you have made for yourself. If you think you are a lion, then you will venture beyond the man-made limitations and embark on the life of the servant leader that you were born to be. That night of the speech, I chose to develop into someone who inspires and influences others within my inherent domain or 'sweet spot'. I believe that all human beings have the potential and capacity to lead. Each of us was created to rule, govern, control, manage, and lead our environments. We are, in essence, leaders, no matter who we are, whether we manifest it or not. For me, I was transformed that night through self-discovery when I understood my inherent leadership potential, who I am, and what I am meant to be. **Self-discovery leads to self-manifestation**. The 20 years since that time have been a progressive process of self-discovery to manifest my real purpose and assignment here on Earth. William James wrote, *'The greatest discovery of our generation is that human beings can alter their lives by altering their attitudes of mind. As you think, so shall you be.'* Centuries earlier, King Solomon, the wisest and richest man of his day, essentially said, *'as a man thinks in his heart, so he is.'* What a person thinks in his heart will ultimately come out in his actions. The challenge is knowing how to change one's attitude. If attitude transformation were simple, then many of us would have changed a number of times during our lives."

Jonas paused and Nicole interjected, "Then what is the key to transforming oneself into a servant leader?"

"Most of us are not servant leaders today because, in our hearts, we don't believe that is who we are. My Papa taught me that true leaders discover and understand who they are and what their purpose is, they influence their environments and cultures more than their cultures influence them. **Servant Leadership is simply influence.**

Everyone has influence; what matters is the kind of influence. Papa offered me this legacy and I was too blind to see it. Papa's legacy is to live out who we are and who we were meant to be, and to influence the culture around us from our unique 'sweet spot'. We must do this regardless of our status, occupation, or even feelings about our leadership ability and potential. Nicole, every human being on this planet has an inclination toward servant leadership; most of us do not have the courage to cultivate it. We have been so conditioned by discouragement, failure, or even the oppression of others that we are afraid to follow our natural servant leadership instincts. When I made the decision to cultivate the intrinsic potential to serve, a transition occurred. I was born to lead by serving. I took the first step and embraced the very reason I came to this planet. Since then, I have progressively manifested all that I was meant to be and do."

Nicole pondered what Jonas was saying and realized that this interview was not just a meeting for a story, but a divine appointment to be confronted with Papa's legacy.

6 THE INNER STENGTH

Nicole was having a hard time keeping her mind fixed on her role as a reporter and caught herself drifting off into the deep places of heart and soul that had gone untouched for many years. Jonas Nolan was hitting a deep chord that was causing her to come face to face with questions that she had been repressing and thoughts that, to be frank, scared her.

"Why are this man's words having such a deep effect on me?" Nicole started to feel her face go flush with that question, but she fought back the feelings and tried to keep her composure.

"I must keep focused on the task, be professional, stick to the facts. Don't get caught up in emotion; get the story and get out!" Nicole's inner talk was like a verbal recording going off in her head.

"Why I am I struggling with these simple words? Am I, too, like the lion coming to the river and being confronted with the truth of my life? Am I playing it safe and not really willing to open up the inner closet of my life? Am I living in fear? If I am, what or who am I afraid of? Am I really living out my 'sweet spot'? I am loosing it, I have drifted off into my own thoughts!" Nicole tried to distract herself by looking at her notes and then back at Jonas, but the flood of questions kept coming back.

"I want to have influence and impact, isn't that why I became a journalist and hopefully…", she stopped with the word *hopefully*. Who was she kidding? "Influence, impact, struggle, and hard work get me nowhere: that's the story of my life. I disappoint everyone: my husband, my kids, and let's not forget dear old dad!" Nicole felt the rush of bitterness hit her at she recalled the memories of her dad and the familiar sense of never feeling good enough.

"Leave a legacy? I am beginning to think no one will even miss me when I am gone!" Nicole shocked herself with that last thought.

"Am I so self-absorbed that I am feeling sorry for myself and giving every excuse for why my life is in such a rut?" Nicole was suddenly startled by Jonas' response.

"Nicole, every human being on this planet has an inclination toward servant leadership; most of us do not have the courage to cultivate it. We have been so conditioned by discouragement, failure, or even the oppression of others that we are afraid to follow our natural servant leadership instincts."

"Do I have the courage to cultivate my own natural instincts?" Nicole pondered.

7 REMEMBER THE "BAMBOO"

Whether you are a grandparent, parent, professional, businessperson, farmer, laborer, etc., everyone leaves a legacy. The question we have to ask is: *what kind of legacy will I leave?*

Jonas restated something Papa had continually shared with him and those who had been impacted by his life. "Consider, if you will: all of us, in one-way or another (good or bad) will have an impact and influence for at least 100 years. Yes, 100 years! The next and future generations need the treasure of our influence. We must not rob generations of the wealth that each one of us possesses. Our influence and legacy is passed down or caught by all we come in contact with and whom our lives intersect, especially your children, grandchildren, and even great grandchildren. It is not necessarily about fame or magnitude of accomplishments, but rather living life with others and as a model for younger generations. What they see modeled, demonstrated, exemplified, talked about, or taught gets planted or embedded in them and passed on to the next generation. I call this "imprinting" or building a total context and culture around the message. The question each of us has to ask is, "What kind of influence or imprinting am I having on others?"

Papa was indeed an amazing man and had a great impact on many different institutions. His personal coaching, mentoring, and teaching of men and women in business, education, and faith-based organizations literally had a worldwide impact. His life and teaching exemplified the axiom he readily shared; *'You cannot teach what you do not know nor lead where you are not willing to go"* Papa was a man who walked his talk.

Nicole asked, "Jonas, could you tell me more about imprinting? I don't think I have ever heard the term used like you just did."

"Papa's heart was to transform cultures one person at a time through servant leadership. In his mind, a culture was any environment in which we are placed where we have influence. Thus, at home, work, or play we can habitually, intentionally, and purposely make a difference. He said it was like breathing. As humans, we need oxygen, therefore, we breathe in the oxygen that brings to life to our bodies. However, we can breathe out carbon dioxide which, for humans, is life threatening in large quantities. Everyone is breathing, but are we habitually, intentional, and purposely pumping oxygen or carbon dioxide into our environments? We can choose the air quality of our cultures by our attitudes, actions, and behaviors."

"So figuratively speaking, the way we breathe does have an

impact on the people in our families, work places, places of worship, schools, etc." Nicole added with a sense of excitement.

"Here I go again, getting emotional...or is his message of servant leadership starting to capture my natural inclinations?" Nicole thought to herself.

"Yes, that's right Nicole. Imprinting is like breathing, but it can be positive or negative. The imprinting we leave on our cultures is done from habits and attitudes that are deeply engrained into our non-conscious mind or what is called the 'heart'. In fact, in the first decade of the twenty-first century, neuroscientists were studying the effects of negativity on the brain. The brain is geared to respond, adapt, and protect, therefore, it's very sensitive to negativity and will take it and internalize it. If people perceive a threat, it activates the 'flight, fight, or refreeze' response. The patterns or habits of mind are primarily slanted toward the negative. Assaraf & Smith, 2008 reported a research study that stated by the time *the average person is 17 years old, they have heard 150,000 times "No, you can't!" to 5,000 "Yes, you can!" a 30:1 ratio toward the negative."*

"Wow, no wonder most people are so negative and down," Nicole commented.

"Negativity breeds negativity and we certainly do have negative cultures. I can't remember where I heard this statistic, but the average elementary school child receives ten negatives comments to one positive every day, a 10:1 ratio. On the other hand, to reverse one negative it takes five positive comments. Again, as you can see our environments are polluted by negativity."

Jonas finished this last statement and noticed Nicole's body language. She was leaning forward and absorbing every word.

"Jonas, with so much negativity in our cultures, how do we positively imprint?"

"The simple answer is that we use our attitudes to positively transform that culture one person at a time though our conversations, interactions, and relationships. Papa used *"The Bamboo Story"* to provide a visual story to create a mental framework that challenged and motivated others to reflect on their current reality and to provide a vision for cultivating a change-ready growth culture through servant leadership. The phrase *"remember the Bamboo"* is like using a key word that immediately triggers the brain's information of what must be our focus of attention individually, at home, in teams, and organizationally as servant leaders.

The Story

Bamboo farmers in Malaysia, using primitive tools and methods that have been passed down through oral tradition for generations, grow a very valuable strain of bamboo that takes great wisdom and patience to cultivate.

•Year 1: The focus of the farmers was on removing the hindrances from the soil that would impede growth. Therefore, they worked twelve hours a day working the soil and removing the impurities and hindrances using the five senses: feel it, see it, taste it, hear it, smell it. When the soil is the perfect consistency the famers plant the seed, water, and fertilize. (At the end of year one, there is no visible

growth or yield.)

•Year 2: The farmers continue to remove the hindrances from the soil, but this year the focus was on moisture content. In year two, framers are working the fields 24/7. Therefore, the precipitation comes either naturally or they irrigate. (At the end of year two, there was no visible growth or yield)

•Year 3: This year, they go back to the procedure of year one. Farmers work twelve hours a day with the focus on removing the hindrances from the soil using the five senses (At the end of year three, there is still no visible growth or yield.)

•Year 4: In year four, the farmers go back to the procedure of year two. The major focus is on the moisture content, working the field 24/7. (At the end of year four, there is still no visible growth or yield.)

•In year 5: This is the year for tremendous growth in just the first 30 days. How much growth? Did the crop grow in inches or feet? It is not nine inches in 30 days, not nine feet, but 90 feet in 30 days! The wisdom and patience of the bamboo farmers yields miraculous growth in year five.

"Jonas, please explain this story, I'm not sure I grasp the connection to imprinting?" Nicole eagerly questioned as she sat back and crossed her legs.

"Nicole, the moral of this story in cultivating and nurturing a positive growth culture through imprinting has several points:

•Remove the hindrances to growth.

David Rock, author of *Quiet Leadership,* reminds us of this simple formula: $\mathbf{p = P - I.}$ Performance (small p) equals our potential (capital P) minus our interference (capital I). People's fears, imagination, self-doubt, self-image, false thinking, etc. get in the way of growth personally and organizationally. Therefore, first and foremost, we must ask, *"What are our hindrances or interferences to growth personally and organizationally?"*

•Cultivating a positive growth culture takes time and great patience.

The change literature talks about transformational change happening in 3-5, 5-7 years. NeuroLeadership (brain-based leadership) research underscores the mindfulness research through focused sustained attention progressively over time. If we focus our attention, we become or take on the characteristics of what we focus on. This is not a microwave process, it is more like a crock-pot, and it takes time to cook.

•The soil (people/leaders) needs a strong and deep root system.

Cultivating a positive culture of service and humility helps servant leaders to focus attention on habit development through empowerment, equipping, and relinquishing control. *"You can not teach what you do not know nor lead where you are not willing to go."* It is character driven from the inside out. It must go deep before it grows wide.

•The Bamboo farmers believe the bamboo will grow and they are committed to the process.

The process of transforming a culture happens one person at a time as their soil is nurtured, cultivated, and hindrances to their growth are removed. Servant leaders must believe and be committed to the process. It is through the process of serving that growth happens because it is "more caught than taught".

• **Remember that growing bamboo, (a change-ready growth culture of servant leaders) will happen progressively through improving the leadership thinking.**

Again, David Rock, author of *Quiet Leadership*, wrote *"They [organizations] need to instill in their leaders and managers the ability to transform performance by improving their thinking...[they] become compassionate about improving not what people are thinking about, but the way they think."*

Nicole, when we choose to focus our attention on equipping and empowering people to maximize their leadership potential and attend to a model and process that best allows those values and beliefs of the culture to be cultivated and nurtured, we are building a total context of imprinting where there is consistency between our beliefs, our actions, behaviors, interactions, and relationships."

Nicole stopped Jonas at this point and asked, "Are you saying that the reason there are negative cultures is because people choose negativity and in reality they have the power to change not only themselves but their cultures?" It was almost as if those words moved in slow motion from her lips so that she had time to reflect on each of them. "Do I choose negativity, really?"

"Yes, that is exactly what I am saying. As I mentioned, a formula for unleashing potential goes like this: performance (small p) equals Potential (capital P) minus Interference $(\mathbf{p = P - I})$. All of us have tremendous potential but something interferes to stifle that potential and make fear or doubt a powerful reality. We all have interferences like: self-doubt, self-image, negative experience, childhood messages that focus on the "cannots", bad habits, misconceptions, dysfunctional thinking patterns, and the list goes on and on. The only thing that really limits our potential is the interference that holds us back. That interference is deeply rooted in our thinking, our mind-sets, our beliefs, our attitudes, and ultimately it impacts our actions. John Maxwell, in his book *Talent is Never Enough*, exhorts:

> *"To reach your potential, you must first believe in your potential, and determine to live way beyond the average. It's one thing to believe that you possess remarkable potential. It's another to have enough faith in yourself that you think you can fulfill it. When it comes to believing in themselves, some people are agnostic. That's not only a shame; it also keeps them from becoming what they could be."*

What we believe on the inside dictates what we are on the outside. Until we come to the point where our personal urgency level drives us to believe what is really true about us, nothing will change. Our personal breakthroughs begin with a change in our own mind-sets or habits of mind. Zig Ziglar, a popular speaker and writer stated, *"Your attitude, not your aptitude, will determine your altitude."* Whatever personal limitations we place upon ourselves are a direct reflection of our beliefs about ourselves. Human potential is limited because we may have a sheep's mentality instead of a lion's. We don't listen or hear the inner voice of potential calling out from within us. Our outward behavior and actions will reflect the inward conditions of our 'heart'. Perception can become a person's reality. We all have to ask, are we being paralyzed by our wrong perceptions and beliefs about ourselves? Do we hear an inner voice shaped by the words and actions of significant people in our lives that have been barriers to our own personal growth and development?"

Nicole's face lit up, as she had a moment of insight. "So what makes servant leaders different is that they don't focus their attention on the interferences, but rather on their potential to serve others. They, to a certain extent, get over themselves and their own 'scar tissue' and focus on others. They are the bamboo farmers who cultivate their cultures! They imprint by their lives through their attitudes, words, and behaviors."

"Nicole, what you just articulated is the heart message of Papa's legacy and in turn gives every human being the dignity and authority to make a powerful difference in this world at home, at work, or at play. Servant leadership is a simple message lived out by ordinary people in extraordinary ways."

"But Jonas, I have to be perfectly honest, is it really that simple? I hear what you're saying, but I know in an hour or two or even tomorrow I'll be back to my daily routine and what we just talked about will seem vague or distant to me personally." For the first time her internal dialogue was now being exposed, and instead of an interview question, this was a personal heart-felt question.

Jonas leaned forward and looked straight into her eyes, noticing that her tone had changed. "Nicole, it all begins with a choice and sense of urgency to be changed or transform. You have to want to change it! Do you want to change?"

"Change IT? Change what? Where do I begin?" Nicole shot back in a knee jerk type of reaction.

8 THE CHANGE "IT" PROCESS

"Nicole, that's a good question: where do we begin?" Jonas repeated the question for effect. He wanted to explain the process as thoroughly and as simply as he could.

"Papa developed something he called *The DEREK Leadership Assessment Profile*™. The word *derek* in Hebrew means your unique way. It is a simple tool he used with those who where seeking to grow both personally and professionally as servant leaders. I have adapted the process and love it because it is so simple. There is genius in simplicity. Papa used to say, *"you don't really know something well enough if you cannot make it simple."* His research focused on helping a person identify his or her leadership thinking and potential. His original research question underscored *"what distinguishes and separates leaders from followers?"* After hundreds of profiles, the overwhelming conclusion was simple but obvious *"the way they think."* Thus, the tool uses a series of six assessments in three domain areas: **Strengths, Passions, and Drives.**

The profile summarizes the individual's unique leadership

thinking. It creates a mirror that facilitates the process of personal change by reflection, mindfulness, and focused attention through what the person identifies as his or her 'IT'. It is about habit development in a personal leadership mind-set. However, Papa, felt that just receiving the profile was not enough, it only created a mirror, the person had to do something with what he/she was seeing or it was just information. Thus, the major part of the DEREK is the 'The Change IT Process'. It was designed to probe into what 'IT' is that needs to change and/or what it is that needs to be developed or strengthened through a series of self-discovery questions. Again, the NeuroLeadership research and specifically the work of Dr. Jeffery Schwartz on mindfulness through self-directed neuroplasticity (the brain's ability to recognize itself by forming new connection through experience) is important here. His work gave us the 'hard' science for what was happening in the transformational process of the leadership thinking and those who were confronted with the servant leadership challenge. Each person moves toward greater insight and cultivates a personal focus of attention. The profile helps the individual realistically see where he or she is currently and then plot a course for where they would like to be as a leader."

Nicole was quick to formulate her next question; "So this process helps people to see their 'IT'! I understand the concept, but how does it help bring about change in a person's life? How do you change 'IT'?"

Jonas stood up and pointed to his head, "The non-conscious

mind is where all of our habits reside, both physical and mental. Think about learning to ride a bicycle. You have to learn to keep your balance on the seat, start peddling, steer using the handlebar, and try to stay in a straight line. As the wheels start the bicycle movement, balancing yourself between the two wheels is difficult. At first you're very conscious of every movement, awkward, and then you loose your balance and fall. However, over time you learn the feel, the sequence of how to balance and peddle. Before long, you have learned how to ride a bicycle, master it, and in time, ride a bicycle without any thought. We walk, tie our shoes, speak in one or several languages, type on computers, ride bicycles, and drive cars, all without conscious thinking."

"Habits (good and bad) are what you create when you do something over and over, to the point where you no longer need to think about it consciously in order to repeat the process perfectly. All of this applies not only to things we do physically, but also our thoughts. When we think the same thing over and over, it becomes a habit of thought. A habit of thought over time becomes an attitude or belief. There is nothing as powerful as attitude. Attitudes dictate our responses to the present and determine the quality of our future. Attitude can simply be defined as our 'mind-set' or mental conditioning that determines our interpretation of and response to our environment. It is our way of thinking. Our attitude is a natural product of the integration of our self-worth, self-concept, self-esteem, and sense of value or significance. In essence, our attitude is the manifestation of who we think we are. We live our lives based on who we think we are."

"I have tried, too many times, to change a habit, lose weight, quit smoking, and even to be a better person, but over time I fall back into my hold habits and get frustrated and discouraged," Nicole added with a discouraged look.

"This is exactly the point of where this conversation is going. How do we change our 'mind-set' or mental conditioning? In order for change or transformation to happen, the urgency level must be high, compelling, and realistic for the individual. In other words, the urgency level must be strong enough to motivate our conscious mind to commit to action. Nicole, please answer this question: *Five frogs sat on a lily pad. One decided to jump off. How many were left on the lily pad?*"

"Is this a trick question? I guess four frogs were left." Nicole hesitated, questioning her answer.

"The question is really not a trick question. Most people will analytically reason the correct answer is four. Unfortunately, the correct answer is not four, but five! All five frogs are still sitting on that lily pad. Why? Because only one decided to jump off, however, he only decided to jump he didn't actually jump. The conscious mind may make decisions, imagine something, ponder an idea, plan something, make a new resolution, or even decide to jump off the lily pad, however, it doesn't mean that we actually will do any of the above.

Neuroscientists tell us that our actions get done through our non-conscious mind. In fact, only two to four percent of our brain functioning is under the control of our conscious mind. The conscious mind can exert control, but only for the short term. The conscious brain has severely limited processing ability. If you find this hard to believe, consider this: the average person loses focus every six to ten seconds. How many numbers in a random sequence can you remember? Think about the last time you called 411 or directory assistance for a phone number. After you hung up, were you able to remember the area code plus the number with out writing them down? Can you remember them now? Our conscious brain has a very difficult time remembering all ten digits, in fact, the research has found that on average it is difficult to remember more than six or seven digits or more than two or three events at a time. While your conscious brain can't possibly keep track of all that, your non-conscious brain can, and it does, nonstop, twenty-four hours a day, every day of your life. If your conscious brain loses focus about every six to ten seconds, how often does your non-conscious brain lose focus? The answer is, NEVER! Therefore, the power center of our brain is in the non-conscious mind."

In order for change or transformation to happen the urgency level must be high, compelling, and realistic for the individual. In other words, the urgency level must be strong enough to motivate our non-conscious mind to commit to action that will ultimately impact our conscious choices. Like the five frogs on the lily pad, it is not enough to decide; we must have an urgency level that forces us to make a committed action toward a preferred future. Most of us can't break certain habits or create new ones because we don't have the right thoughts and attitudes that will enable us to change. Our convictions determine what is stored in our hearts, and our heart is the container of our attitudes. It is like a bank account that we draw from that determines the way we live our lives. We become what we learn, listen to, see, hear, and experience. Our non-conscious mind or heart attitude affects our conscious perceptions and mind-set. In other words, the height to which our heart aspires depends on the information that is in it. We will never rise above our mental conditioning or bar that we have set for ourselves. We can either be our own worst enemy or our own greatest ally. Our perspective is being shaped by our internal belief system, and our internal belief system will either take on a victim's mentality or victor's mentality. Whatever is stored in our heart determines what we think about ourselves and what we believe we can accomplish."

"I'm sure, like myself, nobody wants to be a victim, so how do we use this change IT process tool in order to really be transformed?" Nicole was thinking about her own personal journey and how she had fallen into the victim mentality trap and used it as an excuse or way of rationalizing her behavior and actions.

"I feel like this guy is reading my mind, who is he?" Nicole wondered.

"The Change IT Process is a tool that uses 'mindfulness'. NeuroLeadership researchers and practitioners have underscored the power of mindfulness in changing habits and behaviors. Mindfulness is to be fully present, aware of thoughts, emotions, or actions of yourself and others. It is 'knowing yourself' by being aware of what and who is affecting your thoughts, emotions, behaviors, and actions. Dr. Jeffery Schwartz, in his revolutionary work with OCD (Obsessive Compulsive Disorders), has been extremely successful treating his patients without the use of traditional treatments or the use of drugs, using a four-step mindfulness method. By helping people with OCD through the four-step process of relabeling, reattribution, refocusing, and revaluing, he found that they could actually rewire their thinking process and modify their disposition toward OCD. Therefore, the Change IT Process assists in helping a person identify their 'IT', what needs to be changed or developed, and to focus their mental process by paying attention and self-regulation which are natural functions of brain networks. Dr. Schwartz and physicist Dr. Henry Stapp linked what is called The Quantum Zeno Effect (QZE) with what happens when close attention is paid to a mental experience."

> *"The mental act of focusing attention stabilizes the associated brain circuits. Concentrating attention on your mental experience, whether a thought, an insight, a picture in your mind's eye, or a fear, maintains the brain state arising in association with that experience. Over time, paying enough attention to any specific brain connection keeps the relevant circuitry open and dynamically alive."*

"Thus, QZE eventually hardwires and makes physical changes in the brain's structure or creates a habit or a new mental map. Simply, whatever we intentionally and purposely focus our attention upon, we become. So like the OCD patients, the Change IT Process gives us a framework so we can focus our attention on what we recognize as our 'IT'. We do this through the process of relabeling our 'IT' (identifying the thought, the habit, emotion, the behavior, etc.), reattributing (realizing the intensity and/or interference of the 'IT'), refocusing (focus of attention on a desired thought, habit, emotion, behavior, etc.), and revaluing (to see your 'IT' at face value and not allow it to be an interference)."

Nicole had a glazed look on her face. Jonas, in an apologetic manner continued; "Nicole, I was so focused on explaining the Change IT Process that I may have gotten too technical in my explanation. My daughters have often told me I sometimes go too deep and they get lost in the details."

Lost in her thoughts Nicole was finally able to muster some words, "Actually, it was very interesting, and I think I understand the process. The Change IT Process is a way of identifying whatever 'IT' is for me and to purposely, intentionally, and habitually focus my attention on what change I want and need to make."

"Wow, you have an amazing ability to take complex concepts, and make them simple. Papa would have been the first to encourage and praise you for your insight and ability to simplify my complex answer," Jonas replied with a chuckle in his voice.

"Papa was a man who always took time to fill others' buckets!"

"Oh, here we go again! What is filling buckets?" Nicole smiled as she questioned Jonas.

9 THE 30 DAY CHALLENGE

The vast majority of us don't give or receive anywhere near the amount of praise that we should. As a result, we're much less productive and in many cases, completely disengaged at home, work, and play.

"According to Nobel Prize—winning scientist Daniel Kahenman, we experience approximately 20,000 individual moments in each waking day. Each 'moment' lasts a few seconds. If you consider any strong memory—positive or negative—you'll notice that the imagery in your mind is actually defined by your collection of a precise point in time. And rarely does a neutral encounter stay in your mind—the memorable moments are almost always positive or negative. In some cases, a single encounter can change your life forever."

"Many years ago, Papa read a book that captivated him and made a life–changing difference in his interactions with people: How Full is Your Bucket by Tom Rath and Donald Clifton. Papa would say that this book is a book everybody should read and he recommended and gave it to just about everyone he encountered. The premise is based on what they called The Theory of the Dipper and the Bucket.

> *"Each of us has an invisible bucket. It is constantly emptied or filled, depending on what others say or do to us. When our bucket is full, we feel great. When it is empty, we feel awful.*
> *Each of us also has an invisible dipper. When we use that dipper to fill other people's buckets—by saying or doing things to increase their positive emotions—we also fill our own bucket. But when we use that dipper to dip from other people's buckets—by saying or doing things that decrease their positive emotions—we diminish ourselves.*
> *Like the cup that runneth over, a full bucket gives us a positive outlook and renewed energy. Every drop in that bucket makes us stronger and more optimistic. But an empty bucket poisons our outlook, saps our energy, and undermines our will. That's why every time someone dips from our bucket it hurts us.*
> *So, we face a choice every moment of every day: We can fill one another's buckets, or we can dip from them. It's an important choice—one that profoundly influences our relationships, productivity, health, and happiness."*

Papa would put this into perspective by asking others to think about the greatest recognition they had received. Without question, it causes us to feel better about ourselves and changes even the way we view the person who gave you the recognition, praise, or genuine compliment. Now think about the greatest recognition you ever received in the workplace. Chances are, it caused you to feel better about your organization and, in turn, become more productive. Genuine recognition, praise, compliments can immediately transform a workplace. Just one person can infuse the positive feel of the culture into the entire group by habitually, intentionally, and purposely 'filling buckets'. For that matter, genuine compliments can transform our homes, our teams, and our relationships one person at a time. Bucket filling is an extraordinarily powerful but simple servant leadership strategy. Why? Because, basically, everybody knows how to give a compliment, show appreciation, praise an individual, and provide encouragement. The problem is we just don't do it often enough and consistently."

"Wow, it is amazing how such a simple strategy like bucket filling can have such a transformational effect on people," Nicole gestured excitedly as she spoke. "However, if that is true, why don't more people practice bucket filling?"

"I sound like a school girl who just made the cheerleading squad," Nicole thought as she struggled with her need to be more professional.

"Nicole, again you have asked a great question. Why don't more people practice bucket filling?"

Jonas sat down again and looked directly into Nicole's eyes and said, " Most of us want more positive emotions in our lives and all of the research indicates 99 out of 100 people want to be around positive people; 9 out of 10 report being more productive when they're around positive people. Unfortunately, wanting a more positive culture isn't enough. As we have talked about earlier, most of us have grown up in cultures where it's much easier to tell people all the wrong things they have done instead of praising them when they succeed. I believe that this negativity–based approach in most cases has evolved unintentionally; it, nevertheless, permeates our societies at all levels. Parents, families, schools, and for that matter organizations and companies function on an unwritten rule: *'Let's fix what's wrong and let the strengths take care of themselves.'* Our mindset is basically hard-wired to catch people's weaknesses rather than build on their strengths. Instead of celebrating what makes us unique; we push to 'fit-in' or not to 'stick-out'. It breeds negativity because we become focused on what's wrong and not what's right with others. Those messages are not necessarily always mean spirited in nature, but they contain a negative message of no, don't, stop, fix-it, get better, try harder, and the list goes on and on. It takes five positives to erase one negative. Again, it is no wonder we have such negative cultures."

"Jonas, I feel so convicted thinking about how I immediately judge or criticize people. I never thought about how I have unwittingly drawn from other people's buckets and in reality was contributing to a negative culture." There was so much more she wanted to say about how she treats her family and especially her father, but she was still holding back.

"There is power in our words," Jonas quickly interjected.

"People can make you who they want you to be, if you accept their words into your life. If you hear something long enough, you can begin to believe it. If ideas overwhelm you, eventually you might embrace them and store them in your non-conscious mind or 'heart'. Thus, we become the thing people say we are, if we accept what they say. Once we believe something, we have a different experience of life, because now we react to life out of those beliefs and habits that are hard-wired into our heart (non-conscious mind). In other words, we see more through our beliefs or "frame of heart" than we do through our physical eyes. Therefore, our philosophies, mental frameworks, and habits of thinking are even more powerful than sight, because we interpret what we see with our eyes through the filter of what we believe in our frames of heart."

"So, I am the product of the words and messages I have accepted and ultimately adopted as my own. I can choose to change not only myself, but others around me by filling others' buckets," Nicole spoke with a sense of conviction, but it still sounded like more of a question rather than a bold statement.

"Nicole, Papa tapped into something that everyone could do, but they just need to build a habit of giving genuine compliments, encouragement, and/or praise to people consistently, intentionally, and purposely."

"Now, you have me just where you want me don't you, Dr. Nolan?" Nicole chuckled. "You want me to ask you: how do you build bucket filling into your life?"

"I'm glad you asked," Jonas gave an approving nod and laughed.

"Every opportunity Papa had to interact with a group of people either in a class, workshop, seminar, or even one-on-one somewhere sometime he was going to spring the 30–day challenge."

Nicole looked at Jonas with a quizzical look, "The 30–Day

Challenge, what does that have to do with bucket filling?"

"Papa was a master at creating a sense of urgency for change and then assisting people with simple strategies that they could personally own. The 30–Day Challenge is a strategy that Papa used, and by the way, I also use to give people a framework to build a habit. According to the research, it takes 21-30 days to begin or break a habit. Therefore, if we want to habitually, intentionally, and purposely be bucket fillers, we have to make a habit of giving genuine compliments, praise, and encouragement."

"Nicole, for the next 30 days, I challenge you to give one genuine compliment. Praise or encourage your family, friends, co-workers, colleagues, students, etc. Just one genuine compliment every day for 30 days!"

"One compliment a day doesn't seem that hard; will it really have a transformational effect on my sphere of influence?"

"A genuine compliment, encouragement, and/or praise is more difficult than you might think. A genuine word isn't about outward appearance like 'you look great', or 'I like your dress', etc. A genuine word of encouragement, praise, or compliment focuses in on their character or internal disposition. For example, 'I appreciate your thoughtfulness in helping me with my packages.' 'You are very kind.' Or something to this effect, 'Nicole, you are one of the most open and transparent reporters I have ever met. You have a way of disarming and making others feel comfortable in your presence. I really appreciate how you listen and value what I have to say.'"

With a tear forming in the corners of her eyes and a lump in her throat, Nicole said, "I am deeply touched by your words and admittedly uncomfortable. I am not use to hearing such a heart-felt compliment. I think I could live off that one for a very long time."

"I sincerely mean every word," Jonas added. "There is power in words to build up and free us and also to tear down and keep us trapped in bondage. Genuine words of encouragement are not always easy but anyone can do it. The key is being consistent, frequent, and of course genuine. Here is what happens when we intentionally purpose to give words that build-up and fill buckets, just like the theory states, your bucket also gets filled. If we make bucket filling a habit then not only will you be filling others buckets, but yours will also be filled. The beauty of this strategy is that you don't have to start an advertising campaign for bucket filling, have extensive training in how to fill buckets, or even have to spend any money. It all begins with you giving to others what you yourself would want others to give to you."

Papa and I have kept a file of letters we received from people who took the 30-Day Challenge. Jonas went over to a filing cabinet and pulled open a drawer filled with file folders and each of them contained hundreds of letters. He took a couple of minutes to pull out a few of those letters and began reading them to Nicole.

An elementary school teacher wrote:

"My main focus is to use bucket filling with all students but especially students of lower socioeconomic backgrounds. These students experience drama, despair, and depression daily by those around them; they eventually become part of the continuous cycle. The first step when filling a student's bucket is to take the time to get to know each student. This allows me to give praise or recognition that has meaning for an individual student. I am very thankful that our principal allows us the first two weeks of school to build the foundations of a learning community and gain rapport with our students. Secondly, the praise that I give needs to be genuine. Children know better than anyone else when a compliment is given falsely. False compliments can, in turn, have a worse impact on a child's outlook and it also compromises their trust in you. Thirdly, I need to be aware daily of defining moments that can change a child's life forever.

A high school teacher reported:

"I have learned that my curriculum can only be successful if my classroom environment is conducive to learning. All my student's buckets must be full and so must mine, in order for learning to take place. We must all be in the right frame of mind, before we can learn. We must all be mentally healthy. I found that I can continually beat my head up against a brick wall in frustration or I can get to the root of all my issues. We can create the best curriculum in the world, but if our buckets are not full, it is simply a bunch of paperwork and busywork."

A young woman who took the challenge exhorts that even a child can be a bucket filler.

"Who would of guessed that this simple concept of filling someone's bucket could even have an affect on the youngest of lives. I had the opportunity to explain the meaning of bucket filling to a 7 year old when asked, "What are you reading?" Within minutes, that 7-year-old was explaining bucket filling to her 10-year-old sister and they were filling each other's buckets immediately… The ideas are not profound or newly discovered, yet when meditated on and put into practice, you realize the

positive impact you can have on the people and the world around you. Change starts with one person at a time and I desire to be a person of change. I will forever be a bucket filler!"

A woman shared how bucket filling has changed her life and now she is intentionally filling others' buckets:

"We had a family dinner the other night, and I invited a cousin who none of us have seen in a long time. He is sort of "a black sheep," in the family, and I was uncertain how he would be received and how the dinner would go. It turned out to be one of the most enjoyable family dinners we have ever experienced. I filled this cousin's bucket by inviting him and allowing him to feel wanted, as did the rest of my family. In return, he told us great stories and filled other family members' buckets who needed some attention."

A therapist explains the healing power of positive encouragement:

"I have a client at work whom I've developed a good therapeutic relationship with. She began by telling me that she is a bad person, described her many flaws, and stated that she does not like people. Rather than focus on her faults, I looked at her strengths and began building on those. I have watched this woman physically change from the inside out. She now smiles and speaks more positively about herself and others, and is beginning to work toward positive goals in her life. It makes me feel very happy that I have been filling her bucket, and she also fills mine..."

A high school teacher tells a story of how bucket filling impacted nor only her life but one of her students:

"Coming from a dysfunctional family myself, I learned firsthand how important positive bucket filling could be from a school setting. My dad was an alcoholic and my mom was always negative and moody. My dad passed away 5 years ago, but the co-dependency and negativity are still

present with my mom. School was the one place, besides my grandparents' house, that I felt free and hopeful. I blossomed at school because of consistent, positive feedback from my teachers – this is the main reason I went into education in the first place.

Many kids experience negativity and inconsistency at home due to dysfunctional families. These kids are the ones who most need positive encouragement at school.

Here's a story about a sophomore boy named Donald in my class first semester. Donald lives with mom, but is mostly being raised by grandma. His appearance is a little rough and he wears his pants so low that he looks like a penguin walking around. During the first week of school, Donald and his friend Brian tried to fight another student, Caleb, in my room three times during 7th bell. I had spoken with all 3 privately and asked the principal to move Caleb to my 1st bell – this way it would show that I wasn't trying to get rid of Caleb, just move him to a different atmosphere.

She refused and said, "It doesn't matter where I move Caleb he will find a problem with anyone." Brian ended up dropping and moving into an at risk program at our school, which helped calm Donald down a bit. Every day Donald would come into class and tell us all how he was going to fight some kid, knock someone down the stairwell, hang out with his friends, hint at drinking or doing drugs, etc. He saw a picture of my dog on my desk and told me I had better watch out because he was going to kill my dog. One day I would come home and see my dog dead in the yard. The class, which was a varied mixture of college prep, general, special education students, and thugs looked at him then back at me with jaws dropped in horror. I just took it with a grain of salt and joked with Donald that he shouldn't take his anger out on my innocent dog and that dogs were good companions because they never say anything mean to you.

One day after school he used my phone to call home for a ride. He ended up cussing out his mom and demanding that she drop what she was doing and come pick him up! I talked with him a bit about talking to his mom that way and reminding him that she took care of him when he was little, fed him, changed his diapers, made him cookies etc. He said, 'She didn't do none of that! My grandma took care of me!'

Over the next few weeks, I established a positive rapport with Donald. I even joked in front of the class about Donald saying he was going to kill my dog and he laughed to. When I make blueberry muffins at home I always save him one and brought it by his homeroom in the morning. I sometimes give him gum or candy from my bottom desk drawer. When he stops by, I usually use the opportunity to encourage him to stay away from drugs and sex. He just smiles and says, 'I know.' I tell him 'We don't need any little Donald's running around just yet — give it a few years.' He laughs and says, 'Yeah — ones enough for now!'

These random acts of kindness really did fill his bucket. He still had in school suspensions and Tuesday/Thursday schools on a weekly basis for various misbehaviors — cussing out teachers, skipping class, etc. I was amazed that he still came to school every day.

I didn't have Donald in class 2nd semester, but he came by to visit between classes and even said 'I don't know why I didn't do any work in your class, but I'm going to sign up for it next year.' Sometimes he would try to stay into my next bell and want a pass. I commended him for asking for a pass trying to do the responsible thing so that he could stay out of trouble, but I needed to set boundaries with him. We decided that I would issue a pass for him once a week to stay into the bell a few minutes longer and I told him it was important for him to go to his other class so he could earn the credit. I'm convinced that Donald must have had other positive bucket filling experiences or he would not have continued to come to school."

"Jonas, I am so overwhelmed that such a simple truth can be so transformational. These letters are living testaments to the power of words and being a bucket-filler. I am getting a clearer picture of what your Papa means when he says, 'to serve is to lead.'"

"Nicole, by the way, I was serious about *The 30–Day Challenge*. So, when are you going to begin?"

Jonas and Nicole laughed so hard their sides began to ache.

10 HUGGING AND CORRECTING

The hardy laugh was good medicine for Nicole's soul. She couldn't remember the last time she laughed so hard and so long. It brought a sobering reality of how mindlessly she was moving through life and not enjoying it. A curious thought came to her, "Jonas, the way you describe your Papa, it seems like all he did was encourage, praise, and compliment people around him. Don't get me wrong, I am not criticizing, but he seems, ugh, too good to be true…"

As Nicole paused, Jonas' mind wandered to a very vivid memory of an encounter he had with Papa.

Jonas was a sophomore in college and was home for Christmas break. During his breaks he would try to spend as much time with Grammy and Papa. He had just finished the football season and was unloading to Papa about his coach.

"He is the worst coach I have ever had. He doesn't listen and he picks on me constantly. I think I'm going to quit. I can't take this anymore. In fact, I am better than most of the guys he puts in the game before me. I just can't believe how unfair he is," Jonas pacing and wildly waving his arms complained.

Papa sitting down calmly replied, "Tell me more about your coach and how you feel he has been unfair."

"He plays favorites and he allows guys with inferior ability to play before me. He just won't let me play! Papa, it's not fair! He just doesn't like me." His voice started to crack and tears formed in his eyes.

"Jonas, have you told your coach how you feel?" Papa questioned.

Wiping his eyes and trying to get his composure, "No, I know he won't listen. He just wants to make my life miserable. Papa, he is trying to ruin my football career."

"Jonas, you are not going to like what I have to say to you, but you need to hear this…Stop acting like a two year old!" Papa said sternly.

Those words coming from Papa were like an electric jolt through his body. Needless to say, Jonas was not happy with Papa and the look on his face was one of astonishment mixed with anger. "Papa you just don't understand!"

"Jonas, the problem isn't with your coach, but with your attitude. You are blaming and pointing the finger at the coach, but the first place we all have to start is with ourselves," Papa quickly replied. "You're just taking his side and not trying to see it from my perspective," Jonas pouted and lashed back.

"Listen, we are all very self-centered, and we demand that everything and everyone around us meet our needs. A two year old is like a dictator. It's his way or the highway. He cries, he screams, he hits, he bites, etc., until someone sees it his way. Most of us never get past our twos because we are basically selfish. You are making everything about you. Two year olds want what they want when they want it and most of the time they ant it right now. You need to see that in life when you focus every circumstance, situation, or encounter on your own needs, the world always feels and looks unfair. The most significant choice you will ever make is to stop being selfish and grow up. Jonas, I love you, but you need to grow up."

As Jonas came back to reality, he looked back at Nicole and said, "Papa would be the first one to tell you he wasn't perfect, but he knew how to hug and give correction."

Jonas shared with Nicole his recollection of the memory he had just had about Papa.

"Not immediately, but eventually I recognized the power of what Papa was trying to do during that time. Papa was a hugger and corrector. He knew how to fill buckets, but at the right time he knew how to correct and put you on the right track.

"I understand hugging and correcting, but how does this all fit with servant leadership?" Nicole interjected.

Jonas stood and slowly and reflectively paced, "Servant leaders know how to meet the legitimate needs of people and not their wants. If we meet everyone's needs and wants we just keep them, figuratively speaking, as two year olds. If we give two year olds everything they want, ultimately it will be harmful, dysfunctional, and toxic to their growth. Meeting every need or want only squelches his or her growth. There is nothing sadder than to see an adult still kicking and screaming about everything that doesn't go their way. Servant leaders meet legitimate needs that enhance and empower them. Some of these legitimate needs are encouragement, appreciation, consideration, esteem, trust, honesty, caring, and the need to be heard. They build trust through caring, connection, complimenting and then appeal from trust through conveying wisdom, completing, and correction. Building trust means filling buckets and appealing from trust means to earning the right to speak into a person's life when they need direction to help them get balance and priorities right, and to correct them when they are off path." Jonas walked to his desk and found a notebook and pulled out a chart.

"Papa called this the 6Cs of Coaching from Trust." He held

6 Cs of Coaching from TRUST

	Coaching Skill	Key Idea	Practice
Cultivating Trust	Caring	Servant Leadership "People don't care how much you know until they know you care."	Intentional time (formal & informal)
	Complimenting	Encouragement Filling people's buckets becomes top priority!	Genuine compliments (power of words)
	Connecting	Listening & Empathizing The art of listening and asking questions.	Understand before being understood (effective communication)
	Conveying Wisdom	Developing Character Lead others to their potential.	Moral Leadership (beliefs & values) (modeling & example)
Appealing from Trust	Completing	Integration Personal & Professional	Holistic Balance (Life Action Plan)
	Correcting	Confronting with care Engaging in Healthy conflict	Truth & Humility (tools for conflict resolution)

up a chart and started to explain it to Nicole.

"Caring is loving people by our actions not just our words. Papa would always say that love is the most misused word in the English language. He felt, like others, that our word 'love' is used in so many ways that it almost becomes cliché. In fact, the word love is most commonly used as a noun, but Papa felt that the real understanding of the word comes as a verb. Love is a verb. We love by our actions. He would say, 'people don't care how much you know until they know how much you care.' Love is intentional action in your formal and informal interactions with people. Nicole, how do you spell LOVE?"

By now, Nicole had been well practiced in Dr. Jonas' questions and was a little hesitant to answer, "I don't know, but I am sure you're about to tell me."

Jonas chuckled, "Papa and I when we speak have taken the time to asks groups this question and you would be amazed at the answers we have received. How do we spell love? S.E.R.V.A.N.T.S"

"That is interesting, but I guess by now it should have been what I expected from you and Papa," Nicole quickly added.

"Nicole, S.E.R.V.A.N.T.S. is an acrostic that Papa created to conceptualize love in action in all arenas of life. I still use his Servant Leadership Assessment Process™ to help leaders self-evaluate and to gather input and feedback from family, friends, peers, direct reports, and supervisors, like a 360° evaluation through a series of questions that correspond to the following:

S1 Self-Control (Patience with self & others or "IMPLUSE" Control)

E Encouragement (To give others attention, appreciation, and common courtesy through kindness.

R Respect (To treat others as important people, give others dignity.)

V	Value (By meeting the legitimate needs of others not wants.)
A	Authentic (To be authentic [literally humility, to be the "true" you], not arrogant, boastful, or prideful.)
N	Never hold Resentment (When wrong or wronged, forgive, don't hold grudges.)
T	Trustworthy (To be honest and free from deceptive behavior.)
S2	Stick to Your Commitments (Stick to the choice(s) you have made.)

"Sounds like this tool can be very valuable not only for self-reflection, but to get honest feedback from those who know you best or interact with you on a day-by-day basis." Nicole thought immediately to how the people in her life would evaluate her in the way she displays love in action. She wasn't sure if the results would be something she could handle right now.

Jonas continued, "The second 'C' is for genuine complimenting. We have already talked about bucket filling and giving genuine compliments, encouragement, and praise.

The third 'C' is connecting. This is the art of listening and asking questions. Papa emphasized that is why God gave us two ears and one mouth, so that we would listen twice as much as we talk. In communication, when we have dysfunctional interaction or miscommunication it usually boils down to really hearing what the other person is trying to say. For the servant leader, listening is a way of life and must become a prominent habit. Papa taught the 70/30 Rule. The rule is simple, seventy percent of the time listening and asking questions and thirty percent talking, giving advice, or explaining. He said, the art of connecting with people is listening and asking questions. In order to be understood, we first must understand. The only way to understand is listen and ask questions.

"So the servant leader builds trust through caring, complimenting, and connecting. He/she focuses on others first through their actions and through intentional interaction gets to know the other person and really connects with them." Nicole energetically summarized what Jonas had just shared.

"Nicole, again you have a way of synthesizing complex truths in such a succinct way!"

"To build trust we really have to take the time and effort to focus on building relationships with people. Our lives are so busy we forget what is most important. In all of our relationships, building trust is intentional and requires us to purposely think of others before ourselves."

"You said, after you build trust then you can appeal from trust. Can you explain the rest of the chart?" Nicole was asking this question not so much to understand, but hopefully as something she could personally apply.

"Appealing from trust means you have earned the right to probe more deeply or step into some one's life to help them make adjustments. Conveying wisdom is speaking truth into a person's life and appealing to their character. Socrates said, 'we don't know how crooked a line is until we have a straight line next to it.' Speaking truth into a person's life is always a way to help them find 'straight lines' to measure themselves against. We earn the right to talk straight to the heart. The next 'C' is completing. It is helping a person to find balance in all areas of life both personally and professionally."

"Do you find that most of us are out of balance?" Nicole sheepishly asked, knowing the answer for her.

"Most of us are living in dualism. We separate our lives or compartmentalize. We have a professional life and a personal life. However, we are always just one person. What Papa taught was living life holistically from the inside out. What you do is not who you are, but who you are will always impact what you do. Most of us are living life, but not really living the maximum life that we were created to enjoy. We are living by our "to do lists" and not by our priorities. As the old TV commercial proclaims, 'Life just comes at you, fast!' If we don't live by our priorities and try to focus on life balance, everything and everyone else around us will reflect that. It's about helping people move from reactive to proactive, from unfocused to focused. Servant leaders want to help others to live a life that counts both personally and professionally."

"How do you help an individual or group move to become more holistic and have life balance?" Nicole looked up from her notes and questioned Jonas. She was feeling uncomfortable. Right now, she knew her life was not only out of balance but a mess. She related immediately to the concept of living in dualism. She was thinking, "Can Jonas see right through me and know that my personal life is at a point of crisis?" Nicole felt a flash of warmth move from her neck upward, her face was flush as she became more and more self-conscious.

"Nicole, let me give you an analogy that was one of Papa's favorites called the Juggler's Theory. All of us have 24 hours a day, seven days a week. The key is not the amount of time we have, but how we use the time we have. Life is like juggling. Each of us have many dimensions in our lives, and throughout our lives these will shift and demand attention at different levels. Let's say that we can break down all of life into seven dimensions, or for our purposes: juggling balls. Each of these seven balls can be labeled with the letter 'F.' (Faith, Family, Fun, Fitness, Friends, Finances, Firm [career].) As you are juggling these seven balls, you realize that it is really difficult to sustain all seven at one time. Therefore, over time, one, two, or three can be handled efficiently and effectively. However, all seven will need your attention at various levels depending on circumstances or situations. The question then becomes: how do you know you are juggling the right balls?"

"Now take the analogy one step further: let's just say that these seven balls can be either rubber or glass. If you drop a glass ball it breaks, drop a rubber ball and it bounces. The key is always balancing your glass balls because if they fall you have a mess. Our task in life is to clearly identify our glass balls and keep them in sharp focus. These are our priorities that must not be dropped."

Tears streamed down Nicole's face. Jonas had just hit a nerve. She knew that not only was her life out of balance, but one of her stated glass balls had fallen and was broken. "I feel like a mess; my relationship with my husband and children is so out of whack!", she was crossing the invisible barrier of her role as reporter and a human being who needed to hear and heed what this man was telling her. She put aside her pride and let her reporter walls down.

"I say they are my top priority, but I spend 70-80 hours a week doing my job. I feel like such a hypocrite. I love my husband and children, but in reality it is just words; my actions don't measure up. They are getting the leftovers and most of the time I am not really present even when I am with them."

Jonas gave her a tissue as he heard the muffled crying and sniffling. He waited in silence as Nicole started to regain her composure. He softly spoke, "It all begins with a choice. You can choose today to really make them your top priority."

"How can I do that so quickly? I don't think you understand how complicated my life is." Nicole snapped back with weeping emotion.

"Nicole, the last "C" is correcting. I know you have only interacted with me over a short period of time, but if you trust what I have been sharing with you and the openness about my own life, then, if you will, let me give you some gentle correction."

"I don't think I am going to like what I am about to hear. But I feel like I can trust you." Nicole knew she was at a real crossroads and everything she had been hearing was now bringing her to this moment.

"Nicole, first I want you to know that I am deeply concerned about what you just said and how you expressed it. It sounds like you are really hurting internally about your family. However, you will never find peace and balance in life until you make the sacrifice and commitment to live by your priorities. If you work 70-80 hours a week and you spend as much time as you do focused on your job, you will never be a servant leader; you'll be a person who exists and just muddles through life."

Nicole looked down and shook her head in acknowledgment as she sobbed into the tissue. In time she wiped her eyes with the tissue and took a deep breath. "I know you are right, but I need help changing my way of thinking and my habits."

Jonas, hearing Nicole's response pulled his chair closer to her, sat down, and said, "I want to offer something to you that I think will be helpful. Papa, many years ago wanted to help people like you and I to experience life balance. He, too, was a self-professed workaholic. In fact, he openly shared how he almost lost his marriage to Grammy during the seventh year of marriage because he was so career focused. He was out saving the world and in a flash he was losing his wife and family. Through time, he developed a process called The Priority Management Process™. It is a "mindfulness" tool that guides a person or group through a step-by-step process of personal reflection, collecting personal data, priority development activities, and personal accountability that lead to the *One Day Priority Planning Challenge*. The one-day challenge is for at least an eight-hour time commitment that cannot be home, office, or familiar work meeting places! The goal of the one-day challenge gives the participant focused time away from their familiar environment. This helps facilitate self-directed focus and reflection in self-discovery and personal insights about priorities both personal and professional in order for them to create their own **Ideal Week** based on those priorities. In other words, scheduling from their priorities and making those priorities personalized with clarity and focus. After their planning day, the participants practice their *Ideal Week* for **60-90 days**. After 60-90 days participants prepare their **S.MA.R.T. Action Plans and Reflection.** The whole process takes about five months to complete."

"So it's not a quick fix!" Nicole exclaimed. By this time she had regained her composure, wiped her eyes, and put her glasses back on.

"Oh no! It is a lot of hard work, but it certainly is worth every minute that you invest in the process. But it all does begin with a choice. A choice to change and to really live by your priorities."

Nicole looked up at Jonas and with a smile said, "I guess I have not just heard about hugging and correcting, I experienced it from one of the best huggers and correctors around."

"You have such a way with words," Jonas chuckled.

11 SERVANT FIRST

"The servant-leader is servant first...It begins with the natural feeling that one wants to serve, to serve first. Then conscious choice brings one to aspire to lead." Robert K. Greenleaf, Servant Leadership: *A Journey into the Nature of Legitimate Power & Greatness*

Jonas went back to the kitchen to refresh their coffee and refilled both cups. The smell of the freshly poured coffee filled the office. Nicole was thinking about the simple words, "it begins with a choice." It was hard to get her mind around all of this. She had to probe further not for the story, but to pursue answers to her own personal life journey.

Nicole sipped her coffee and looked intently at Jonas and asked, "How do you identify a servant leader? How does one tell a truly giving, enriching servant from a person whose net influence is to take away from or diminish other people?"

"That is a really interesting question," Jonas replied as he tried to blow on his hot coffee before his next sip. "We live in a complex, institution-centered society; there will be concentrations of power both large and small. Power can used for the common good, but many times in institutions it will be coercive power used to dominate and manipulate people. The servant leader uses power to create opportunity and alternatives so that individuals may choose and build autonomy. He/she uses authority to serve the individual for the common good. There are those who use coercive power overtly and sometimes brutally to manipulate others. Others may use coercive power more covertly, but the intent is the same. Most of us are more coerced than we know or are willing to admit. The problem with coercive power is that it strengthens resistance. When leadership is, to some extent, manipulative, it is successful at controlling, but the effects only last as long as the force is strong. However, over time human beings will either actively or passively rebel against coercive manipulative control. This kind of power has been around a long time and its effects have been seen historically in every form of institution imaginable.

Servant leaders use their authority not to coerce, manipulate, or control, but to equip and empower people to act and behave as those who are fully human. Servant leaders have power, but their power is not used to hurt or control; rather it is used to cultivate for the good of the individual, and in turn for all."

"Jonas, what you are proposing seems to be exactly the opposite of what traditional concepts of leadership promote and spread through entire cultures and the thinking of companies and organizations: the belief that leadership is about power and control." Nicole added.

"The world teaches that leadership is controlling and imposing one's will on people. But that is not leadership, only control! It is really manipulation and dictatorship. Servant leaders serve the needs of others and act in accordance for the good of people. Over 30 years ago, Robert Greenleaf wrote a monumental work, Servant Leadership, in which he rightly pointed out the misconceptions of the word 'institution' and its negative connotations in our modern society.

> *I have studied the etymology of the word (institution) it does have a rather checkered history. Tucked away in the many historical meanings is 'something that enlarges and liberates.' Can you think of another single word that has that connotation? We have habit in this country, when something goes wrong; to abandon the word that names it. Wouldn't it be a better idea, if we have the right word, to change the offending practice and keep the word? I want to keep the word institution and build a far greater substance in what that word refers to. Let me suggest a definition for our purposes: 'An institution is a gathering of persons who have accepted a common purpose, and a common discipline to guide the pursuit of that purpose, to the end that each involved person reaches higher fulfillment as a person, through serving and being served by the common venture, than would be achieved alone or in a less committed relationship.'*

The traditional pyramid bureaucratic hierarchical structure of leadership common in our thinking and practices cannot and will not unleash this deep seeded intrinsic need to serve and be served. The pyramid structure of leadership in organizational thinking ultimately leads either directly or indirectly to everyone being under the power or control of one person or group of persons. Giving that person or group too much power is really abnormal and eventually corrupting. This leadership structure of thinking gives control the priority over leadership. It feeds the notion that one must be the 'boss' to be effective. Survival becomes the name of the game and sheer performance is considered brilliant. Servant leaders turn the pyramid thinking of leadership upside down."

"Wow, I get what you are saying, and, by the way, fully agree. But what will have to happen to change the traditional leadership thinking and turn it upside down?" Nicole quickly interjected.

"The original reason we were given authority was not to use it on people but to release people. Basically, a selfish person wants all the glory, all the credit, all the power, all the authority, all the rights, and all the privileges. But a servant leader wants to share what he/she has. Nicole, the way to turn the pyramid upside down is to grasp and practice the difference between power and authority."

Nicole nervously smirked, "How is understanding the difference between power and authority going to turn the leadership pyramid upside down?"

Jonas looked Nicole compassionately in the eye and said, "Max Weber, a sociologist at the turn of the twentieth century wrote extensively about institutional and organizational leadership. His definitions of power and authority, taken from his writings, are what most sociologists since that time have acknowledged and use. In fact, these same sociologists, have found a very significant relationship between power and authority. They noticed that as power increases, authority decreases, and vice versa. Oppressing or suppressing others leads to loss for both the oppressor and the oppressed. Weber defined power as 'the prerogative to determine what happens and the coercive force to make others yield to your wishes–even against their own will.' This last phrase is crucial, for the coercive nature of power gives expression to its potential for evil. Power is the strength to command. Ultimately, it sounds like this: Follow me or else!

He defined authority like this, 'When a leader is able to persuade others to do his will without coercion, when he presents himself in such a way that people want to obey him, when they recognize him as a legitimate leader with the right to expect compliance with his wishes, I say that he has authority.' In other words, this is the right to control, command, or determine. A power or right that has been delegated or given, an authorization: authority is the right to lead. This happens when those who follow are willing to give a person control or command out of deep respect and trust. Authority sounds like this, "I choose to follow you."

"So, are you saying that throughout history coercive power has ultimately destroyed and suppressed the potential of multitudes of people? And this oppression is found in every institution, organization, and workplace as long as we view leadership as power and control?" Nicole was more restating than asking a question. This insight was alarming to her, but she could see it not only in history, but in her own personal experience in schools, religious institutions, workplaces, and of course her own family.

"So how does true authority work to cause change from the traditional leadership focus on power?" Nicole questioned with intensity.

"Nicole, the true joy of servant leaders is not to see others serve them but to see others discover themselves. True authority releases more authority. Leadership is always transitional. Any leader who thinks that he or she is permanent or irreplaceable will ultimately have to come to the realization that his or her leadership is temporal at best. The greatest mistake, temptation, or weakness is for leaders to think that the world begins and ends with them. The ultimate neutralizing agent—death! Terminal thinking happens when a leader only focuses on the task at hand and not on building the people around them to do the task. When a leader uses power to control, he or she is destined to fail in the future. No matter how successful you are it will all die with you, if you don't pass it on. If your business, organization, family, ministry, or your vision dies with you, you ultimately fail. Success without a successor is failure. The average leader employs other people. The servant leader deploys others. True authority gives authority away to others and is not threatened by their success; in fact it brings them great joy. We should never lead with ourselves in mind, but even more essential is to never lead with only your generation in mind. Succession is always on the mind of a servant leader. He/she is constantly seeking and searching to equip and empower others so that they can serve their gifts to the world and make a difference."

"Are you saying that you can tell true leadership because it produces other leaders who produce other leaders?" Nicole asked as she nodded her head.

Jonas chuckled and his eyes twinkled, "I couldn't have said it better. Servant leaders rejoice in the progress and success of others and ultimately their purpose is to see leaders at all levels as a result of their influence. True leaders do not maintain followers. They produce leaders because they believe that leadership potential resides in everyone around them. Nicole, insecure people with poor self-esteem are afraid to develop people. They need dependent followers to prop them up. They are not really leaders. Servant leaders cultivate an environment for leadership to blossom and grow. A true servant leader creates a culture for others to find their area of authority and unleash them to serve their gift to the world."

Nicole looked down at her notes and was contemplating a very important question, "Jonas, if the vast majority of people are unaware of their intrinsic potential as servant leaders and are easily influenced and to some extent controlled by anyone or anything that is stronger than they are, how is the leader-first power mentality impacting institutions, businesses, faith-based ministries, and even families?"

"Nicole, people are suffering from a form of mental illness."

"Mental illness? What are you talking about?" Nicole shot back like a knee jerk reaction.

"Dr. Myles Monroe, in his book *The Spirit of Leadership*, helped me to understand this condition. I'm not referring to the medical term for mental illness, but I am referring to the wrong thinking that is causing confusion until we experience and find our 'sweet spot', our reason for being born. The result of this condition is self-hatred, self-deception, fear of failure, fear of success, fear of the unknown, distrust for others, a distrust of God, ignorance of personal strengths and ability, lack of destiny, and a survival mentality. Most people don't really live, they just make a living and focus on retirement, and when they retire, they die because they lack purpose and destiny. This mentality leads to only one sure conclusion, and that is death. Everything else is somewhat uncertain. Today, the way people are dealing with this uncertainty and lack of purpose is through medication, either legal or, if necessary, illegal. Nothing is more lethal than power in the hands of one who suffers from this kind of mental illness. This ultimately results in oppression. Dr. Monroe put it this way:

> *"Our leadership today is a product of the thoughts of our leaders, and therefore the saying is true: 'as a man thinks in his heart (subconscious mind), so is he.' When you want to study leaders and their leadership, do not study their physical appearance or demeanor. Study their hearts. Find out where they got their thoughts and ideas. A society generally cannot produce a leader better than itself because that leader usually gets his or her beliefs from the society. Therefore, basically, we appoint people who are no wiser than we to lead and guide us. Every society should*

constantly check the source of the information by which it is living."

Nicole listened intently and contemplated all that Jonas was sharing with her. In the back of her mind, she was relating everything

he was saying back to her own life. This assignment had moved from getting an interesting story to a personal confrontation with truth. This truth was ringing clearly to her now, and she realized that this message needed to be heard by all. True leadership has more to do with our mind-set than with methods and techniques.

12 WILL YOU BE PART OF PAPA'S LEGACY?

Nicole was contemplating her interview with Dr. Jonas Nolan trying to get an angle for her article. The more she reflected the more her thoughts were drawn not to writing an article, but the inner curiosity about her own life and purpose. Jonas had mentioned that people either live by default or destiny. It was a no brainer to Nicole that she was certainly living by default. Life was coming at her fast and at times she felt like she was just a passenger on this ship called earth and really had no say in what journey she was on. Her family had issues, but she knew she was loved. She went to college, started a career, married, and had children, but somehow she felt that something was missing. The "missing" feeling had been bouncing around in her for years, but it wasn't until this interview with Jonas that it all moved to front and center stage. The feelings surfaced like a great wave and she knew that like a surfer she needed to be prepared to ride the wave or be buried by it.

Then it hit Nicole like a ton of bricks! "What am I really missing?" It was an "AHA" moment for her. "I am living by default, my purpose here on earth is not clear. I am letting life happen to me but I am not really living fully alive according to my unique assigned purpose."

Nicole formulated a question and asked, "Jonas, how does a person move from living by default to finding their unique sweet spot?"

"Nicole, are you really asking how you can be part of Papa's legacy?" Jonas' eyes were warm, open, and welcoming as he asked her this question.

"I thought Papa's legacy was for those who desire to be leaders or want to have that kind of influence." Nicole was a little perplexed at Jonas' question and again confronted that inner voice about her own life.

"Papa's legacy is for everyone. In fact, Papa's legacy is a worldwide movement of committed servant leaders of all walks of life who equip and empower people to find and come into their "sweet spot" so that we will transform cultures one person at a time."

"I don't know if I can--" Nicole stopped herself in mid-sentence. She realized she was giving another excuse, but was not sure of how this would happen for her.

"Nicole, I certainly understand your inner conflict. If you remember, this was all a part of my journey. I grew up with a grandfather who lived this legacy and I didn't really have a clue until that moment at the podium at the leadership conference. When I chose to stop living for myself and started serving others. Until that point, as I mentioned at the beginning of this interview, I thought that I was at the center of the universe and realized it was not about me. I came to a crossroad, a moral decision point, when I was confronted with the truth about myself and I needed to do something about it."

"Are you ready to be part of Papa's legacy?" Jonas' expression was challenging, but full of compassion.

Nicole knew after all that she heard to this point, it was now time to make a decision. As she had mentioned before, this was much more than just an interview, it was a life-changing encounter and now she was faced with a choice. Immediately, her thoughts turned to anxiousness and an overwhelming sense of fear started to grip her mind. That anxiousness and fear turned to discouragement as she realized that what Jonas was sharing with her was going to be very difficult, and she had tried to change so many times before and failed. She was fueling her sense of discouragement from her past experience and her past experience was now dominating her thoughts.

Jonas recognizing the symptoms of fear and discouragement interrupted her thoughts. "Fear is a thought that is everywhere. This kind of thinking only attracts negativity and fear. For a person to live consciously or unconsciously in continual dread, cringing, and being downcast by your thoughts will accomplish nothing, but ultimately lead you to lose everything. Nicole, fear, anxiousness, worry, discouragement, and hopelessness are everywhere. People are afraid of public opinion, private opinion, what we are doing today may not be ours tomorrow, sickness, and death. Fear has become for millions a fixed habit. That habit of thinking only leads to discouragement."

Nicole was surprised at how well Jonas had been reading her thoughts and feelings. As much as she didn't want to admit it, her mind was overcome by fear.

Jonas continued, "Real courage is about a person living in his or her sweet spot and through humility serving his or her gift to the world. Remember all of us have a garden to tend. It will not grow and thrive until you choose to cultivate it. Every day that goes by without you fulfilling your sweet spot means countless others are missing out on what you and you alone uniquely serve to the world. When people lose hope, they are no longer productive at a level of maximum potential and effectiveness, which in turn negatively impacts their overall contribution to their family, business, community and their personal and professional relationships."

"I never thought about my life in that light before. I always thought that my choices and my life direction really only impacted me. I never thought about the interrelationship of how my life does influence positively or negatively," Nicole reflectively stated. She was realizing that her thinking and her mental framework of approaching life were engrained, passive, and laissez-faire. It was alarming how much of her mind was dominated by negativity and fear-based thinking.

"Jonas, can you help me find my sweet spot?"

"Nicole, your sweet spot is within your grasp. It is like a seed that has been planted within you that just needs the right soil and climate to cultivate it. In all of creation, one of the most simple but powerful elements is the seed. If I held a tiny seed in my hand and asked you, 'What do I have in my hand?' What would you say?"

Nicole, thought and responded, "Maybe I would say the obvious, a seed! But knowing you, obviously that is a true answer but considering the nature of a seed, I see a plant or flower or even a forest or a garden."

Jonas nodded, "Yes, the ultimate truth is not what you see now, but what it will become. **The seed in itself is not an end, but within this tiny element is the means to what it can become.** In other words, the seed is full of potential. The seed, like your sweet spot, is the place uniquely fitted for each of us where we discover and live out our unique gifts and function in and at our maximum potential. It is the place where you come alive because you are being and doing what you do best and what you were created to be and do!"

Jonas leaned forward as Nicole's head dropped and he positioned himself so that he could look directly into her eyes.

"Nicole, what makes you come alive? Remember self-discovery followed by self-manifestation will set you on a path of freedom from the constraints of culture, society, and other people, so that you can become the leader God intends you to be. You must learn who you are, and then reveal yourself to the world."

With tears in her eyes, Nicole looked up at Jonas and said, "I come alive when I write articles and stories that encourage and motivate others."

"I wonder how many hundreds of people—perhaps thousands or millions—were born or are yet to be born who need to benefit from the books or articles you have neglected to write or continue to postpone. This generation and the next generations need the treasure of your unique potential. Think of the books and great treasure of words and ideas that others in past generations have left for you. Even as their treasures have become your blessings, so your unique talents must become your children's unborn children's blessing. We need the treasure of your potential." Jonas' passion was evident to Nicole and she could feel the zeal of his words.

"No amount of accomplishments can replace the power and the motivation of finding and unleashing your own sweet spot and working toward your dreams. Until we live out of purpose and destiny, our existence really has no meaning. Some people have thousands of reasons why they cannot do what they want to do, when really all they need is one reason why they can. The only thing that will hold you back is you!"

"We have a common vision for the common good. Nicole, you can be part of a worldwide movement of ordinary people who simply live out their purpose and destiny for being born into this world and then in turn serve their unique gifts and talent to the world through the 'garden' where they live, work, and play."

Nicole removed her glasses, and filled with emotion she felt the tears streaming down her cheeks and knew that what she was hearing would not only change her life, but potentially the lives of so many others.

Jonas continued, "We want to transform cultures (work, school, home, etc.) one life at a time. We want to develop authentic transformational servant leaders in all segments of life, race, culture, and nations that transcend all socioeconomic lines and third world barriers. True freedom and purpose are possible only as individuals discover and then are unleashed into their personal purpose and design. Nicole, you must accept the fact that there is something you were born to do that no one else can do with your particular bent or expertise. Will you be part of Papa's Legacy of living an ordinary life to serve others with purposeful, intentional, and habitual influence in the unique way that God has given to you and you alone?"

A prolonged pause and quite a few tissues later, Nicole regained her composure.

Jonas smiled and asked, "What was one of the most defining moments in your life?"

Nicole laughed out loud. Dr. Jonas K. Nolan turned a routine business article interview into a life changing encounter and divine appointment. "My most defining moment in life just happened!"

"Nicole, there is no greater joy than to hear those words from you."

She pondered and in a moment of tremendous insight she said, "Dr. Nolan I know now what my sweet spot that will serve to the world is."

Her words caught his attention, "Tell me, Ms. Demas, what is your sweet spot?"

"I am going to write books that inspire and motivate people to live out their potential and transform the world one person at a time."

"Wow, I know you will do just that," replied Jonas.

"In fact, I have an idea for the first book," Nicole interjected.

"Don't keep me hanging!" Jonas shot back.

"The first book will be Papa's Legacy: A Leadership Parable."

Appendix:
Assessment Tools mentioned in Papa's Legacy

"DEREK" Profiles™

The Hebrew translation of the word "way" is "derek." Derek refers to a path worn by constant walking, and it also can mean a journey. Metaphorically speaking, derek refers to our unique actions and behavior. In other words, way (derek) speaks of the unique imprints that each of us have that are both genetically inborn and the result of our environment.

"DEREK" Profiles™ have been developed to help an individual uncover and unleash his or her potential.

"DEREK" Learning Assessment Profile™ is a tool that uses a series of assessments to create a mirror that reflects learning potential. The profile helps the individual realistically see how he or she learns, processes, and thinks. The individual can better understand how he or she learns and develops skills in learning, thinking, and processing. (In addition, parents and educators can use this tool to better be able to coach, direct, and facilitate learning for their children/students.)

"DEREK" Leadership Assessment Profile™ is a tool that uses a series of assessments to create a mirror that reflects leadership potential. The profile helps the individual realistically see where he or she is currently and then plot a course for who he or she would like to be as a leader. The profile becomes a stepping-stone to start the Individualized Leadership/Life Coaching Plan™ process.

Change "IT" Card™

"Change "IT" Card™ is a simple tool to begin the process of developing habits that are intentional and purposeful to produce transformation personally and professionally. The Change "IT" Card is designed to probe into what it is that needs to change or what it is that needs to be developed or strengthened.

Life Action Plan Process™

What is a Life Action Plan? A Life Action Plan looks at all dimensions of your life holistically and crafts a roadmap for movement in all of those dimensions. We start off by examining seven dimensions of life and identifying your balance in those areas by looking at your priorities. Then we look at areas for habit development that are achievable, inspiring, measurable, and can be shared. The life plan is crafted as a process that has goals/objectives that can be easily communicated.

Individualized Leadership/Life Coaching Plan™

Individualized Leadership or Life Coaching Plan (ILCP) is a process developed and reviewed for each client. While everyone is ultimately responsible for their own personal and professional development, the partnership of the coach provides a significant resource to help the client shape his or her goals and progressively move toward them. This is an important distinction of FutureNow's approach to personal leadership and life action development. The individualized coaching plan is crafted as a process that has goals/objectives that can be easily communicated.

Priority Management Process™

Priority Management Process™ is a basic premise regarding Priority Management: if you don't schedule your priorities, everyone and everything else around you will. If you don't take charge of your schedule, teammates, vendors, solicitors, managers, golf buddies, relatives, and whoever or whatever else will fill your days for you. If you don't identify your top priorities and schedule your day around them, at the end of the day you'll always find yourself using leftover space to cram in what you consider important. And you know the worst thing? That's usually exhaustion time. The Priority Management Process guides you through a step-by-step process of personal reflection, collecting personal data, priority development activities, and personal accountability that lead to the "One Day Priority Planning Challenge."

If you are interested in contacting Mike for any of the above mentioned tools and/or workshops, keynote speaking, or a presentation based upon concepts presented in this book contact him at mstabile@futurenowed.com or visit his website for additional workshop information or services of FutureNow Consulting, LLC at www.futurenowed.com.

References

Assaraf, J. & Smith, M. (2008). *The Answer: Grow any Business, Achieve Financial Freedom, and Live and Extraordinary Life*, Atria Books, Simon & Schuster, New York, NY.

Autry, J., (2001). *The Servant Leader*, Three Rivers Press, New York, NY.

Brady, C. & Woodward, O. (2005). *Launching a Leadership Revolution*, Obstacles Press, Grand Blanc, MI.

Collins, J. (2001). *Good to Great*, Harper Business, New York, NY.

Covey, S. (1991). *Principle Centered Leadership*, Random House, New York, NY.

Covey, S.(1989). *The Seven Habits of Highly Effective People*, Simon and Schuster, New York, NY.

Covey, S. (2004). *The 8th Habit: From Effectiveness to Greatness*, Simon and Schuster, New York, NY.

Covey, S.M.R. (2006). *The Speed of Trust: The One thing that Changes Everything*, Simon and Schuster, New York, NY.

De Pree, M. (1997). *Leading without Power,* Jossey-Bass, San Francisco, CA.

De Pree, M. (1988). *Leadership is an Art*, Double Day, New York, NY.

Edmondson, A. (2008, July-August). The competitive imperative of learning. Harvard Business Review. 60-67.

Glaser, J. E., (2006). *The DNA of Leadership: Leverage Your Instincts to Communicate, Differentiate, Innovate,* Platinum Press, Avon, MA.

Goleman, D. & Boyatzis, R. (2008, September). Social Intelligence and the Biology of Leadership. Harvard Business Review. 74-81.

Gordan, E. (2008). NeuroLeadership and Integrative Neuroscience: "it's about validation stupid!" NeuroLeadership Journal [1] 71-80.

Greenleaf, R. K., (1983) *Servant Leadership.* Paulist Press, New York, NY.

Hassed, C. (2008) Mindfulness, wellbeing and performance. NeuroLeadership Journal [1} 53-60.

Irving, J.A., & Longbotham, G.J. (2007). Team effectiveness and Six Essential Servant Leadership Themes: A regression model based on items in the Organizational Leadership Assessment. International Journal of Leadership Studies [2] 2. 98-113.

Jensen, R. (2001) Achieving *Authentic Success,* Life Coach Foundation, San Diego. CA.

Jung-Beeman, M, Collier, A. & Kounios, J. (2008). How insight happens: learning from the brain. NeuroLeadership Journal [1] 20-25.

Kotter, J. (1996). *Leading Change,* HBS Press, Boston, MA.

Kotter, J.(1999). *What Leaders Really Do,* HBS Press, Boston, MA.

Kotter, John (2002) *The Heart of Change,* HBS Press, Boston, MA.

Kriegel, R. & Brandt, D. (1996). *Sacred Cows Make the Best Burgers: Developing Change Ready People and Organizations,* Warner Books, New York, NY.

Lencioni, P., (2002). *The Five Dysfunctions of a Team*, Jossey-Bass, San Francisco, CA.

Liberman, M. & Eisenberger, N. (2008). The pains and pleasures of social life: a social cognitive neuroscience approach. NeuroLeadership Journal [1] 38-43.

Ochsner, K. (2008). Staying cool under pressure: insights from social cognitive neuroscience and their implications for self and society. NeuroLeadership Journal [1] 26-32.

Maxwell, J. 1993). *Developing the Leader Within You*, Thomas Nelson, Nashville, TN.

Maxwell, J. (1999). *Failing Forward*, Thomas Nelson, Nashville, TN.

Maxwell, J. (2000). 21 Irrefutable Laws of Leadership, Thomas Nelson, Nashville, TN.

Maxwell, J. (2003). *Think For A Change*, Warner Business Books.

Monroe, M. (2009). *Becoming a Leader: Discovering the Leader you were meant to be!*, Whitaker House, New Kensington, PA.

Monroe, M. (2008). *In Charge: Finding the Leader within You*, FaithWords, New York, NY.

Monroe, M. (2005). *The Spirit of Leadership: Cultivating the attitudes that influence human action*, Whitaker House, New Kensington, PA.

Rath, T. & Clifton, D. (2004). *How Full is Your Bucket?* Gallup Press, New York, NY.

Ringleb. A.H. & Rock, D. (2008). The emerging field of NeuroLeadership. NeuroLeadership Journal, [1] 3-19.

Rock, D. (2008). SCARF: A brain-based model for collaborating with and influencing others. NeuroLeadership Journal [1] 44-52.

Rock, D. (2006). *Quiet Leadership: Six Steps to transforming performance at work,* Haper-Collins, New York, NY.

Rock, D., & Schwartz, M. (2006). The Neuroscience of Leadership. Breakthroughs in brain research explain how to make organizational transformation succeed. Strategy + Business. www.strategy-business.com/article/062007.

Schwartz, J., & Begley S. (2002). *The Mind and the Brain: Neuroplasticity and the Power of Mental Force.* Harper-Collins, New York, NY.

Senge, P, (1999). *The Dance of Change: The Challenges of Sustaining Momentum In Learning Organizations,* New York, NY Doubleday-Currency.

Senge, Peter (1990). *The Fifth Discipline: The Art and Practice of the Learning Organization,* New York, NY Doubleday-Currency.

Tang, Y., & Posner, M. (2008). The neuroscience of mindfulness. NeuroLeadership Journal [1] 33-37.

Waters, Lea, (2008). Using human brain dynamics to enhance workplace team dynamics: Evidence from two applied case studies. NeuroLeadership Journal, [1} 61-66.

ABOUT THE AUTHOR

Michael J. Stabile, Ph.D. is an experienced educator, life/leadership coach, consultant, and author. He focuses on equipping and empowering people to influence and impact their cultures. He founded and leads FutureNow Consulting, LLC. FutureNow is committed to personal, group, and organizational transformation through a workshop/seminar approach and/or personal life coaching using customized presentations.

CPSIA information can be obtained
at www.ICGtesting.com
Printed in the USA
LVHW050905250420
654389LV00005B/437